"However 'stuck' or 'unstuck' you might feel at any given moment, participating in Keith and Sandra's insightful and creative book is like having your own professional but personal breakfast club. In just a few minutes I got more than enough good ideas to last a long time." **— David Allen, author of *Getting Things Done* and *Ready for Anything***

"If you are a leader on the up escalator but lack a mentor who can help you navigate the dangers of corporate life, UNSTUCK will provide witty and useful advice. Ideas disguised in different media jump at you from many angles, and if you take the time to reflect on them, you emerge wiser and more energized." **— Mihaly Csikszentmihalyi, professor, Peter F. Drucker School of Management; author of *Finding Flow* and *Good Business***

"Part action manual, part tool, part dojo, UNSTUCK is unfailingly inventive when it comes to tackling the toughest challenges of making strategy, organizing work, and leading people. If you're stuck—and you will be if you aim to do great work— UNSTUCK is a fresh, fun, and serious-minded guide to moving forward." **— Polly LaBarre, contributing writer, *Fast Company*, and author of *Mavericks at Work***

"While we know the attributes of a good team and good direction, we surprise ourselves with how such smart and motivated people can allow dysfunction to creep into our progress. Eureka! Keith and Sandra reveal our vulnerabilities by defining imbalances in our ambitions rather than faults in our character." **— Ric Grefé, executive director, AIGA**

"UNSTUCK really walks its talk. The gems of information, questions, and case studies throughout are take-aways that make you think in new ways." **— Ivy Ross, executive vice president of design and development at Old Navy**

UNSTUCK

A TOOL FOR YOURSELF, YOUR TEAM, AND YOUR WORLD

Keith Yamashita and Sandra Spataro, Ph.D.

PORTFOLIO

PORTFOLIO
Published by the Penguin Group
Penguin Group (USA) Inc., 375 Hudson Street, New York, New York 10014, U.S.A.
Penguin Group (Canada), 90 Eglinton Avenue East, Suite 700, Toronto, Ontario,
Canada M4P 2Y3 (a division of Pearson Penguin Canada Inc.)
Penguin Books Ltd, 80 Strand, London WC2R 0RL, England
Penguin Ireland, 25 St Stephen's Green, Dublin 2, Ireland (a division of Penguin
Books Ltd)
Penguin Group (Australia), 250 Camberwell Road, Camberwell, Victoria 3124,
Australia (a division of Pearson Australia Group Pty Ltd)
Penguin Books India Pvt Ltd, 11 Community Centre, Panchsheel Park, New Delhi –
110 017, India
Penguin Group (NZ), cnr Airborne and Rosedale Roads, Albany, Auckland 1310, New
Zealand (a division of Pearson New Zealand Ltd)
Penguin Books (South Africa) (Pty) Ltd, 24 Sturdee Avenue, Rosebank,
Johannesburg 2196, South Africa

Penguin Books Ltd, Registered Offices:
80 Strand, London WC2R 0RL, England

First published in the United States of America by Portfolio, a member of Penguin
Group (USA) Inc. 2004
This edition published in Portfolio 2007

10 9 8 7 6 5 4 3 2 1

Copyright © Keith Yamashita and Sandra Spataro, 2004
Introduction copyright © Keith Yamashita and Sandra Spataro, 2006
All rights reserved

ISBN 1-59184-037-6 (hc.)
ISBN 978-1-59184-147-0 (pbk.)
CIP data available

Printed in the United States of America
Designed by STONE YAMASHITA PARTNERS (www.stoneyamashita.com) and
ZipFly (www.zipfly.net)

IN YOUR HANDS, YOU'RE HOLDING THE PAPERBACK VERSION OF UNSTUCK.

We couldn't be happier, because the more affordable price on the cover means that more people will have access to this work.

The masterful Adrian Zackheim, our publisher and guide, asked us to write a new preface to the book—to share some of the things we've learned since the original UNSTUCK was published.

And so we sat down to write this preface.

Writing a book is a little bit like a vacation in uncharted territory—you head out in one direction, but it is in the unplanned distraction of what gets discovered along the way where the truly beautiful stuff happens. UNSTUCK has very much been that for us.

WELCOME. Greetings. Good Day.

It has taken us into companies and organizations we would have never had a chance to meet otherwise. It has introduced us to thousands of leaders, teams, and students. It has given us opportunities to run workshops, innovation labs, and soulful conversation sessions with some amazing human beings, of so many different ilk. While we originally wrote UNSTUCK with the idea that it would help leaders in business, we've found out, in dozens of interactions, that the lessons, ideas, and models in these pages apply equally well to people's personal lives too.

But most of all, it's affirmed our belief that getting stuck is simply part of life—if you're not stuck from time to time, in your work, or in your personal life, you're probably not aiming for greatness. All great leaders, teams, and individuals get stuck at some point—it's merely the sign that you're challenging the status quo. Of course, true greatness belongs to those among us who know how to get unstuck.

To keep to Adrian's original request, we're putting forth ten things we've learned since publishing UNSTUCK the first time around in hardcover....

And in typical unconventional UNSTUCK manner, this preface is probably best read after you've read the rest of the book. Either way, have fun with it.

—Keith Yamashita and Sandra Spataro

ALL LEADERS, TEAMS, AND INDIVIDUALS WHO ASPIRE TO BE GREAT, GET STUCK.

THAT SAID, NOT ALL INDIVIDUALS WHO GET STUCK ARE WILLING TO ADMIT THAT THEY'RE STUCK.

(We've been trained to think that getting stuck is a bad thing.)

IF WE WANT MORE PEOPLE TO BE GREAT, WE HAVE TO FIRST ERASE THE STIGMA OF BEING STUCK—SO MORE PEOPLE WILL ADMIT THEY ARE.

WE AGREE WITH THE DOYENNE OF THE AIR-WAVES, OPRAH, THAT THERE ARE ONLY TWO POLAR FORCES IN LIFE THAT REALLY COUNT— *Love* AND *Fear*.

(When we wrote UNSTUCK originally, we didn't realize how much we agreed with Oprah.)

WHEN YOU'RE
OPERATING OUT
OF *Love*, AND
TRULY REACH-
ING OUT TO THE
WORLD, TRYING
NEW THINGS,
AND LIVING
UP TO YOUR

POTENTIAL— THAT'S WHEN YOU'RE MOST LIKELY TO GET STUCK, BECAUSE YOU'RE DEEPLY CHALLENGING THE STATUS QUO.

(Yours, and often, everybody else's.)

THOSE OF US WHO STAY STUCK, DO SO BECAUSE WE'RE PARALYZED BY *Fear*.

WE'VE LEARNED THAT GETTING UNSTUCK REQUIRES STARING OUR FEAR IN THE FACE, AND RELENTLESSLY LEANING INTO IT.

(That's hard work, and most of us are not taught this as kids, in school, or from our early mentors.)

STARING *Fear*
IN THE FACE,
THE CHALLENGE
THEN IS TO FIND
ONE SLIVER OF
OPPORTUNITY
TO DEFEAT
THAT FEAR—AND
OFTEN, THAT
BREAKTHROUGH
IS OUR OPENING
TO GET UNSTUCK.

FROM THERE, IT'S ABOUT SYSTEMS THINKING, SYSTEMS THINKING, SYSTEMS THINKING.

(We're not taught this in school either, yet it's so fundamental to change—you have to pay attention to many individual elements to make the whole healthy.)

THE BIGGEST
LESSON WE'VE
LEARNED IS
THAT GETTING
UNSTUCK
REQUIRES A
KIND OF LEVITY
OF BEING. OR
PERHAPS MORE
SIMPLY SAID:
Have more fun.

And with that, we hope you'll have fun in the following pages....

HOW TO USE THIS BOOK.

IF YOU WANT TO CREATE AN
ACTION PLAN, LOOK AT SOME
PATHS WE SUGGEST. **(GO TO
PAGE 162.)** ▶

RECORD YOUR OWN PATH
AS YOU READ THE BOOK.
(USE PAGE 166.) ▶

YOU'RE READY TO KNOW
MORE ABOUT THE INSIGHTS
BEHIND THIS BOOK—THE
THEORY, THE DATA, AND
THE GOOD THINKERS.
(GO TO PAGE 172.) ▶

WHAT'S IN THIS BOOK?
(TURN THE PAGE.) ▶

This book is for you and your teammates (whether you've been a team for five days or ten years). It's for everybody who wants to push forward when it's not at all clear about how to push forward. We want this book to be a simple, smart, and useful tool—right now. Getting unstuck involves three basic steps, so we've organized this book around them.

Step 1: Admitting you're stuck.
Things aren't going well, and you're coming to terms with that fact. ▸ **Start on page 6.**

Step 2: Diagnosing why you're stuck.
You definitely feel stuck, but you aren't sure why. ▸ **Skip to page 28.**

Step 3: Getting unstuck.
You know why you're stuck, and you are ready to move forward. ▸ **Skip to page 48.**

CONTENTS

Log onto **www.unstuck.com** for tools, more case studies, and leader's guides.

THE STORY
OF UNSTUCK.

Behind every book is a story. This is ours. We are **Sandra Spataro** (a professor of organizational behavior at the Johnson School of Management at Cornell University with a passion for teams, diversity, leadership, and what makes organizations effective) and **Keith Yamashita** (a cofounder of a firm in San Francisco that works with CEOs to reinvent, rejuvenate, and recenter their organizations).

The idea for UNSTUCK came about when Sandy was teaching an MBA course at Yale and invited Keith to teach a few classes with her. The topic for the classes? How to flex leadership and communications skills in complicated times. In preparing for those classes, our ambition was to create a tool that would help the students lead their teams through times of change. We wanted to take knowledge from Sandy's research, other thinkers in the field, and Keith's on-the-front-lines work with CEOs — and bake that knowledge into a form that these leaders could use in tough situations to drive the right actions in their teams.

We soon discovered that while there are thousands of books published every year on leadership, management, and innovation, very few function as in-the-moment tools that let

you take instant action. We ended up creating a set of
flash cards, which we hastily named Unstuck Cards.
And an interesting thing happened. The cards were a hit.
The students demanded more of them. One student even
remarked, "This is the stuff I came to business school
to learn, wrapped up in a way that I can actually use."
We were on to something.

Fast-forward a few months. Keith was invited by the editors
at *Fast Company* magazine to speak about the topic of
change at their annual RealTime conference. Rather than
just create a standard presentation, we decided to create an
entire experience — a book (a compilation of the Yale flash
cards) and a room filled with activity stations and exercises
to help conference attendees make change happen. More
than 250 people participated. We heard things like "I get it.
Finally, a way to get my team's head into the game again."
"This helps me think through why we're not making any
progress." "Hallelujah, there is hope!"

We knew we were on to not just a good tool, but a whole new
way to help organizations get stronger and better at what they
do. And the idea for the book you are holding was born.

Step

1

ADMITTING YOU'RE STUCK.

(Or how to recognize the symptoms.)

BE HONEST. HOW IS IT REALLY GOING?

Stuck? Maybe it's only been for a day. A week. Okay, a month! Get out a pen and write down some thoughts about your symptoms. Be open. Be truthful. After all, no one is reading your answers, and the person who benefits most from your honesty is you.

Just how stuck are you?

▶ Describe the nature and duration of being stuck.

▶ Write down (in full glory) what you're feeling, why you're stuck, why it seems you can't forge ahead.

▶ Are you stuck on something? With something? In something? With someone?

Further things to write about:

▶ What are you trying to achieve?
  (Don't just focus on the end
  goal. Think about your values.)

▶ Can you identify the roadblocks?
  If so, what are they?

▶ Is it just you? Or is your whole
  team in a funk?

Yet more things to write about:

▶ Have you already tried to get
  unstuck?

▶ Who do you have in your realm
  who can help you get unstuck?

▶ Afraid to admit you're stuck?

YOU'RE

STUCK.

It's okay. Really.
All great people get
stuck at some point.
The trick is knowing
how to get unstuck.

NOW, GO FORWARD BY ZOOMING OUT.

You've had some time to think about your symptoms, and you've taken an important first step: **You've started to admit that you might be stuck.** ▸ So, what do you do with that admission? ▸ How can you cut through the fog, the politics, the loss of optimism that comes from hitting a wall? ▸ How can you move forward when everything seems to be heading in reverse? Oddly enough, we find that moving forward often requires zooming out so you can see the bigger picture. Once you see the bigger picture, the actions you need to take become more clear.

You see, in working with hundreds of leaders, we've observed that there is a process they follow to get unstuck:

1. **They diagnose why they're stuck.** Like great doctors, they look at the symptoms to determine what's ailing their team, their organization, and their company. (We'll teach you how to do that in step 2, starting on page 28.)

2. **They are systems thinkers. They get unstuck by rejuvenating different parts of their organization's system.** This is about looking at your organization as a living organism that needs to be fed, inspired, protected, and nourished. To make a healthy organism, you have to put its fundamental systems into balance so the parts are working with each other rather than against each other. Organizations that are out of balance become stuck— unable to move forward. What's more, Darwin might have argued: Those organizations that remain stuck, become dead. (More about "systems thinking" in a moment.)

3. **They get wildly innovative and intensely tactical about activating different parts of their organization's system.** The majority of pages in this book are dedicated to the methods great leaders use to get their teams unstuck. Some of these ways are quirky, while others are common sense. Some are inventive, others are basic. This book is a compendium of these ideas on how to get unstuck; each idea can be powerful if used at the right time.

LEARN TO FIX THE SYSTEM, NOT JUST THE SYMPTOM.

Now you know a little about how great leaders get unstuck, and you're probably ready to charge ahead. But before you do, it's smart to learn a little more about systems thinking. That's because getting unstuck is not merely the act of treating the symptom of being stuck, but rather of getting to the root cause. Or even better, it's about trying to fix the whole system of your company, your department, or your team. To become more effective, you must master ways to help get the system back into balance.

To succeed as a leader (or, for that matter, as an individual), you need to unify:

▷ **Your purpose.** The driving ambition that shapes what you and your organization aspire to achieve and work collectively to make a reality.

▷ **Your strategy.** The smart way you go about achieving your purpose.

▷ **Your people and the way they interact.** The people that are assembled—and rallied—to execute the strategy, and, as important, how they treat each other to get the work done.

▷ **Your structure and process.** How the team is structured— who makes decisions, who is included and who is not, who has authority over whom, who is in charge, who has informal authority (not necessarily a title, but lots of influence). And the formal process (or simply the understood method) by which the team collaborates to get the job done.

▷ **Your metrics and rewards.** The activities and actions that get measured (or at least paid attention to) as indicators of whether your team or organization is delivering on its purpose. Once these are measured, your organization rewards those who've been part of the accomplishment.

▷ **Your culture.** The largely unwritten set of rules that govern behavior—or, as one CEO said to us recently, how work gets done when you don't specify how the work should get done.

It helps to create a visual model of these six elements, and use it to understand where you need to take action.

SEE THE SYSTEM.

This diagram can help you think about what's going right, and what's not, in your realm. It's a picture of a healthy system — the team's essential elements are all in balance. When you're stuck, it's usually because one or more elements have gotten off track. How does this picture compare with what's going on with your team? Is your strategy in line with your purpose? Are you structured to deliver on that strategy? Do you have the right people — and do they work well together? Is it clear what victory is — and do you know what the leading indicators of success look like? To move your team into the success zone, you need to put your system into congruence. That's the road to getting unstuck.

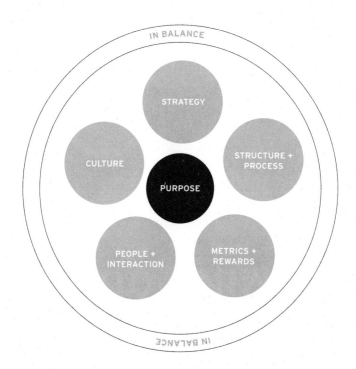

The inspiration for this model came from two primary sources: a classic Friday late-afternoon conversation with former Hewlett-Packard CEO Carly Fiorina, who is one of the more holistic systems thinkers we know; and from David A. Nadler and Michael Tushman, whose work in "A Congruence Model for Organizational Effectiveness" shaped our thinking. **TO LEARN MORE, SEE OUR LIST OF SOURCES, STARTING ON PAGE 172.** ▶

DO ANY OF THESE SYSTEMS GIVE YOU INSIGHT INTO YOUR OWN?

These diagrams show just a few of the ways systems can get out of balance. You might see your situation in one — or even a few — of these. Or your situation might look completely different. Whatever the case, our goal is to help you train your mind to examine your symptoms of being stuck, and determine what might be out of alignment about the system of your team.

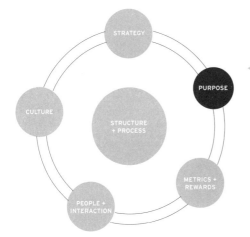

◄ Protocol-crazy
Does your organization value structure (hierarchy, titles, rank, who reports to whom) and process ("This is the way we've always done it.") over anything else? It's protocol over substance. Think DMV.

▶ Off-kilter
Is your organization high-performing but caught in a seismic shift in your industry? Your system may be aligned but aimed at the wrong task. Think Microsoft caught by surprise in the rapid rise of the Internet.

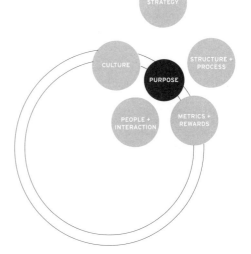

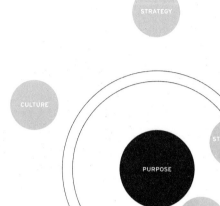

◄ **Discombobulated**
All the right elements
are present within the
system — even a vital
and compelling purpose.
But nothing pulls them
together. Each element
is working against the
others, and the system
is out of balance. Think
about an organization
going through a major
restructuring, or two
firms that have been
recently merged
into one.

▶ **All heart, no action**
Do you have an amazing
purpose, but little means
to act on it? Think about
the not-for-profit with
an important cause, but
lacking the talent or
discipline to execute it.

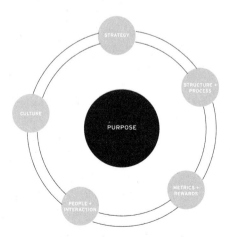

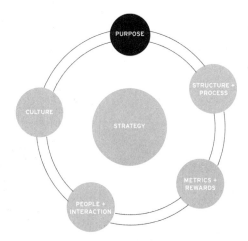

◄ **All brains,
no brawn**
All strategy, but no
ability to pull it off.
Start-ups often suffer
from this ailment.

► **Stuck in your
own lore**
Do you have a culture
so dominant that it has
become impossible
to innovate within it?
Everything is about
preserving what has
been, not focusing on
what could be. Think
megacorporations gone
complacent. Or cults,
for that matter.

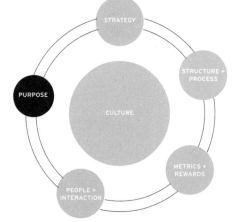

JUST HOW STUCK ARE YOU?

One last diagnostic to determine the severity of your stuckness. Look over your scribbles and notes on the previous pages, then answer these questions:

▸ Do you have a clear, inspiring purpose?

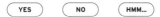

▸ Do you have the right people, in the right positions to make a difference?

▸ Do you work effectively as a team?
   Can you always get the right stuff done?

▶ Does the team truly get the most from diversity — in skills, geography, gender, age, ethnicity — to broaden its thinking?

YES   NO   HMM...

▶ Do you know how to make decisions?

YES   NO   HMM...

▶ Do those decisions stick?

YES   NO   HMM...

▶ Is your team capable of radical ideas?

YES   NO   HMM...

▶ If your team leader quit today, could the team carry on?

YES   NO   HMM...

If you answered no to any of these questions, turn the page to dig even deeper. (By the way, if you answered yes to all of these questions, you're either part of an extraordinary organization or you're deluding yourself. Even the highest-performing teams rarely earn a yes on all fronts.) Looking for even more help? Go to the "Diagnostic Tools" section at www.unstuck.com.

Step

2

DIAGNOSING WHY YOU'RE STUCK.

(Or how to get at the root causes.)

THE SERIOUS SEVEN

Let's move from symptoms to causes. Symptoms vary quite a bit—no two teams feel stuck in quite the same way. But a great majority of "stucks" result from at least one of seven primary causes—what we've termed the Serious Seven. In the following pages, we describe each cause. If you suffer from one or more of the Serious Seven, you'll very quickly recognize yourself in these descriptions. Then, knowing which causes apply, you can craft a plan of action.

OVERWHELMED

EXHAUSTED

DIRECTIONLESS

HOPELESS

BATTLE-TORN

WORTHLESS

ALONE

WHICH APPLY TO YOU? ▶

The Serious Seven No. 1

Overwhelmed

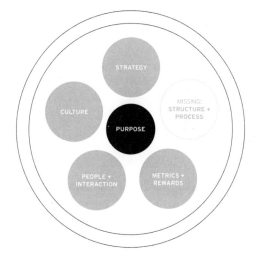

Feeling overwhelmed is most often the result of an organization's lack of structure and process. **TO BEGIN THINKING ABOUT THE PROBLEM, GO TO PAGE 67.** ▶

You're stuck because your team doesn't know what to do next. You used to be so certain about where to go, but here you are now, rudderless. It all seems like too much work. Or you feel like you're under too much scrutiny. Or there are too many moving parts. Or you don't have enough people or time to get it all done.

Tell-tale signs: It's procrastination city. You can't figure out why you can't get started — you may even have many of the elements to succeed, but you're still stuck. The task ahead feels huge.

Sound familiar? ▶ "We know what to do, but we have no idea how we're going to get it done." ▶ "Is it just me, or does the boss look like a deer in the headlights?" ▶ "Failure might not be an option. But it doesn't look like success is either." ▶ "Does it seem like we spend more time talking about how to scale back the project than actually doing the work of the project?"

If left untreated: You'll fail to tap into the great talent of your team. It's like having a car with a turbocharger that never gets used.

The Serious Seven No. 2

Exhausted

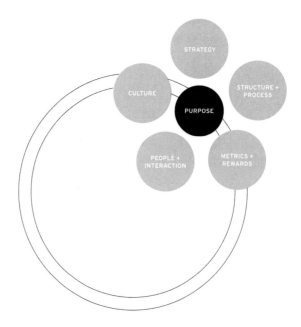

Feeling exhausted most often comes from concentrating on the individual parts of the system, but neglecting to bring them into balance. **TO GET ENERGIZED, LOOK PAST THE EXHAUSTION— AND INVENT A PROTOTYPE OF THE END STATE. GO TO PAGE 115.** ▶

You're stuck because it's been rough sailing recently. Perhaps your original intent — your North Star, if you will — was clear. But as the team sailed on, the sextant was thrown overboard. Once a brilliant crew, the team is now paralyzed by politics, wasted efforts, opinions arising from fear, and even the occasional mutiny. Progress is slowing to a standstill.

Tell-tale signs: Team burnout. Resentment over new projects. Waning interest or involvement in team get-togethers and meetings.

Sound familiar? ▶ "It's not like things are broken, but it doesn't feel right either." ▶ "I'm pooped." ▶ "If it's not one thing, it's another. Once we get one thing fixed, something else springs a leak." ▶ "Have you ever noticed the boss is too chicken to ask for help?" ▶ "Hey, where did all the fun go?"

If left untreated: Exhaustion slowly gives way to cynicism. Shutdown, then backlash, may not be far behind. It's like losing the other runners — and even the course — halfway through a marathon.

The Serious Seven 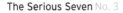 No. 3

Directionless

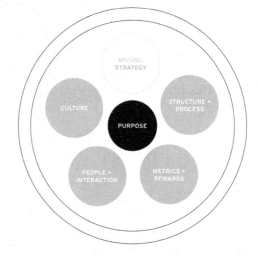

Feeling directionless most often happens when there is a lack of strategy in the organization — or the strategy is out of sync with the rest of the system. **FIX THAT BY FIRST DEFINING YOUR ASPIRATION. GO TO PAGE 51.** ▶

You're stuck because your team is all thrust, no vector. People are busy, but aren't necessarily effective. Everyone is obsessed with their to-do list, yet there is no "big picture" to guide their actions. Decisions are made with little regard for the context of the day — let alone what tomorrow might bring.

Tell-tale signs: It may seem like there's a lot of good action taking place, but there are few tangible results. Often, team members are unable to connect their work to the larger context of what must be done. What's more, judgment calls about what's important often turn out to be wrong later.

Sound familiar? ▶ "I'm so busy, I don't have time to think." ▶ "We get to good, but rarely to great." ▶ "Why doesn't the boss tell us why we're doing this?" ▶ "Luck is our biggest salvation."

If left untreated: The outcomes are often mediocrity and a failure to reach desired goals. The team may arrive somewhere, but it is not likely to be the correct destination.

The Serious Seven  No. 4

Hopeless

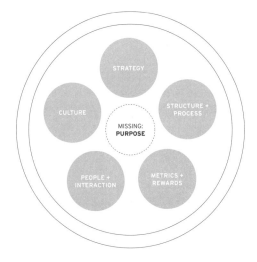

Feeling hopeless is often the result of an anemic purpose.
You might have the other elements to succeed, but without
purpose you have no energy. **TO FIX THAT, USE THE EXERCISE
ON PAGE 51.** ▶

You're stuck because your team lacks a central purpose. A kind of general defeatism has set in. The team is spinning. All the hard work seems like exactly that—just hard work. There is no feeling of reward, no sense of achievement.

Tell-tale signs: Your team used to have tons of passion—but where'd it all go? There's no rallying cry, especially when the going gets tough. It takes an awfully big dose of success to get the same rush you used to.

Sound familiar? ▶ "We have no idea why we exist." ▶ "We all have our own agendas, and no one is on mine." ▶ "I get a certain joy when there's a rumor I'm going to be transferred to a different team." ▶ "I'm outta here."

If left untreated: A lack of inspiration can be contagious. One person's uncaring attitude soon becomes the mood of the group. Before long, motivating your team, rather than doing the work, is how you spend virtually all your time. And you feel like a cheerleader with laryngitis.

The Serious Seven No. 5

Battle-torn

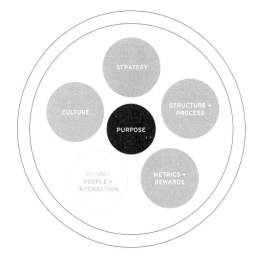

Feeling battle-torn can result from any number of problems with the people on your team and the way they interact. **BEGIN FIXING THAT BY GETTING PEOPLE TO PLAY NEW ROLES IN MEETINGS. GO TO PAGE 99. ▶**

You're stuck because your team can't get along. This syndrome leads to a group so torn by its own foibles that it never even gets to fight the outside enemy. This is friendly fire at its most disturbing. It can bring even the toughest to their knees.

Tell-tale signs: Team members with hurt feelings, bruised egos, or political agendas. Team interactions characterized by unresolved conflict, defensiveness, lack of communication, and high levels of inhibition. Factions, cliques, bullies, and desertions.

Sound familiar? ▶ "We spend more time fighting than working." ▶ "You don't dare speak up in meetings because someone will take your head off." ▶ "Psst. Collude with me, and you'll be okay." ▶ "I never said I'd protect you." ▶ "Emotions are for wimps." ▶ "Let's take this offline." (And all the real decisions are made in the hallways after official meetings.) ▶ "People are only comfortable offering ideas one on one."

If left untreated: The team never turns its attention to the real task at hand. It's like a dysfunctional family trying to throw a wedding.

The Serious Seven No. 6

The Serious Seven No. 6

Worthless

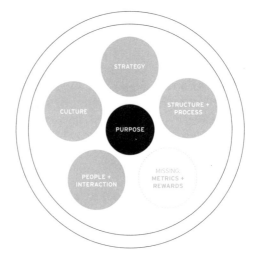

Feeling worthless is often the result of poor metrics (you don't know what leading indicators to watch for) and poor rewards (when you do good work, it goes unnoticed). **START THINKING ABOUT MOTIVATION AND INCENTIVES ON PAGE 68.** ▶

You're stuck because your team is unable to recognize what success looks like. Moving targets. Muddy expectations. The right actions aren't rewarded. Even when the team does something amazing, it's overlooked. Before long, the team feels its contributions don't matter.

Tell-tale signs: You don't know what victory looks like—so you wouldn't know if you achieved it. The metrics of performance seem vague. Team members are puzzled over which goals to pursue. Management has little credibility—when they request that work be done, employees don't always listen. Commitment wanes.

Sound familiar? ▶ "The boss asked me to do this. Should I even bother?" ▶ "Do you think when they said it was due Friday they meant Friday?" ▶ "It seems like we're all just going through the motions." ▶ "Okay, I'll do your project—but what will you give me if I do?"

If left untreated: Team members spend their time thinking up ways to sabotage progress—except for the few martyrs who continue working when neither the expectations nor the rewards are clear. Imagine a whole team of Dilberts.

The Serious Seven No. 7

Alone

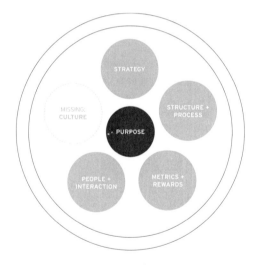

Feeling all alone is often the result of a lack of a cohesive culture—the team just doesn't have its own religion to unify everyone. **TO SEE THE LIGHT, LET YOUR SOUL BE YOUR GUIDE AND START ON PAGE 75. ▶**

You're stuck because the team has lost its own religion.

It used to feel like a close-knit unit, but somewhere along the way the sense of belonging was replaced by the haze of an identity crisis. Your crew lacks a culture to unite it, so it is far less than the sum of its parts.

Tell-tale signs: Individual team members make up their own rules. The team never seems to be in sync. Every meeting feels like the first time the team has worked together. Lots of new leaders pop up, but they don't seem to last very long.

Sound familiar? ▶ "Unless the boss tells us what to do, nothing gets done." ▶ "New team members can't seem to master the ropes." ▶ "It's just chaos, chaos, chaos." ▶ "You can get away with pretty much anything you want."

If left untreated: The costs of coordination go through the roof. The group has no natural pattern of success, and methods are invented anew every time. Visionary leadership is replaced by the need for command-and-control authority. "Herding cats" doesn't even begin to describe it.

WHICH OF THE SERIOUS SEVEN APPLY TO YOU?

The wheel at the right suggests paths you can follow to get unstuck. Feeling particularly overwhelmed? Follow the page numbers we've suggested. Feeling battle-torn? Follow the pages suggested for that. Feeling worthless? Well, you get the idea. Each collection of pages represents a journey. Along the way, you'll be given lots of relevant examples, ideas, and tools. That said, you can start virtually anywhere in the next section of this book—just look at the bottom of each page for where to go next. No matter which method you choose, enjoy what you do. (Remember: This is the fun part. Getting unstuck can be liberating!)

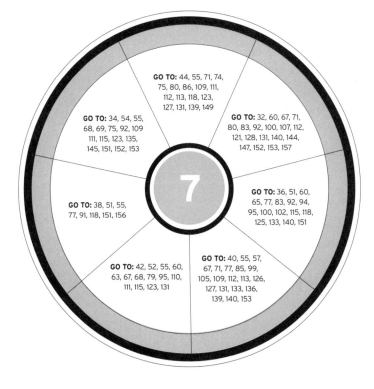

GO TO: 44, 55, 71, 74, 75, 80, 86, 109, 111, 112, 113, 118, 123, 127, 131, 139, 149

GO TO: 34, 54, 55, 68, 69, 75, 92, 109 111, 115, 123, 135, 145, 151, 152, 153

GO TO: 32, 60, 67, 71, 80, 83, 92, 100, 107, 112, 121, 128, 131, 140, 144, 147, 152, 153, 157

7

GO TO: 36, 51, 60, 65, 77, 83, 92, 94, 95, 100, 102, 115, 118, 125, 133, 140, 151

GO TO: 38, 51, 55, 77, 91, 118, 151, 156

GO TO: 40, 55, 57, 67, 71, 77, 85, 99, 105, 109, 112, 113, 126, 127, 131, 133, 136, 139, 140, 153

GO TO: 42, 52, 55, 60, 63, 67, 68, 79, 95, 110, 111, 115, 123, 131

The Serious Seven—and what you can do to combat them. Pick the word that best describes your current condition, then use the tools on the pages listed above.

IF YOU WANT A MORE STRUCTURED PATH OF ACTION, TURN TO PAGE 162. ▶

Step

3

GETTING
UNSTUCK.

(Or what you can do right now.)

The following pages are filled with tools, techniques, and examples to help you get unstuck. There are many paths you can take. Start here, and work your way through in a linear fashion. Or turn back a page, and follow our wheel. Or pick a random starting point and go. Any page with a tool icon in the upper corner suggests something not just to think about, but to do. Along the way, we've cited useful readings and sources; you can see a full list on page 172.

Have a moonshot.

Teams are formed for many different reasons—some more glamorous than others. What can you do when the purpose for your team is clear but not obviously inspiring? Ponder how your team's contribution ultimately affects the world. Humble acts often add up to major differences.

Look at what your team does and ask: "Why do we do what we do?" Ask the question again about the answer you give. Then again and again until you get to an answer that has meaning.

Strong teams have a purpose—a driving ambition to achieve something worth doing. Try this exercise: Write down your answers to the following questions. Why do you exist? What must your team accomplish before you consider yourself a success? What is your contribution? The answers should define your purpose—why you do what you do. Purpose gives your team the clarity to act, and the passion to weather downturns. A clearly expressed purpose can give investors confidence that you know what you're doing. It can give the press a lens through which to report about your actions. And it can give your partners something to rally around.

Bonus exercise: How do you know if you've articulated your true purpose? Can you recount it in the time it takes to ride an elevator from the lobby to the penthouse? If so, good. If not, keep working. Brevity can help breed clarity.

DO YOU FUTURECAST? (PAGE 60) ▶
DOES YOUR BRAND REFLECT YOUR PURPOSE? (PAGE 151) ▶
DOES EVERYONE CARRY THE VISION? (PAGE 123) ▶

Trust is a bank account. Invest often.

And withdraw wisely. Trust is often what makes a good team great. Interactions based on trust free the team from incredible drains on both energy and resources. Trust minimizes politics. Trust prevents having to hoard information, question other teams' agendas, suppress wild ideas, or otherwise indulge in such time-wasting activities. The secret?

Stress the similarities among members; there is trust in common bonds.

Lose in the short term to gain in the long term; think twice before you violate the trust you've built with a colleague.

Increase face-to-face contact, at least while members are still forming relationships.

Make people accountable for actions that hurt the team.

Designate times to evaluate group process and participation; don't let the trust account go bankrupt before calling a meeting about it.

Trust is one of the cornerstones of a team that uses passion and emotion to advance its own productivity.

To master the topic, read "Building the Emotional Intelligence of Groups" by Vanessa Druskat and Steven Wolff. This article highlights techniques to promote positive interaction and build trust.

IS THERE TRUST AT THE CONTROL POINTS? (PAGE 145) ▶
DO YOU TRUST THE TEAM'S INNOVATOR? (PAGE 73) ▶
DO YOU FOSTER TRUST WHEN YOU SPEAK? (PAGE 86) ▶

CASE STUDY: EMBRACING CHANGE

If you think your organization is exhausted, consider the United States Postal Service. Dating to 1781, the USPS is older than any U.S. company. It faces the constant challenge of ever-faster, on-demand expectations (think email, express delivery, online tracking). How does this large entity respond—and avoid giving in to exhaustion? For one, it embraces the competition. In 2001, for example, the USPS formed an alliance with FedEx—the express carrier renowned for speed and reliability. FedEx now transports express mail, priority mail, and limited first-class mail for the USPS. Under this partnership, dependability and speed (words rarely used to describe the U.S. mail) became an instant offering.

OVERCOMING FEELING EXHAUSTED
Take-aways: (1) Embracing change is a key to growth. (2) Think creatively about how to use the competition to your advantage.

More heart, less intellect.

Appeals to the soul are based on emotion, which was a dirty word in business until not that long ago. Recent research on emotional intelligence is showing that acknowledgment and the expression of emotions—in an appropriate manner— can contribute to productivity in groups.

Have you established safeguards for showing emotion and passion on your team?

Most of us are trained to be logical. When given a problem or roadblock, we try to dig into the facts. Determine a path based on data. Argue our case using data. And when that isn't working, pile on more data. Often, motivating teams to take the right action requires first doing something else entirely: spending time building a common identity, or picking a common enemy, or gaining a common understanding. Getting unstuck involves appealing not just to your team's rational mind, but also to its soul.

NO HEART? START WITH A NAME. (PAGE 77) ▶
CONSIDER GROUP DYNAMICS. (PAGE 112) ▶
CAN YOU ARTICULATE YOUR THOUGHTS? (PAGE 83) ▶

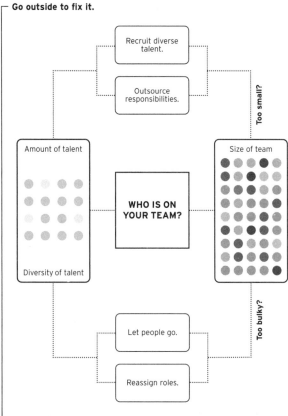

Go outside to fix it.

Recruit diverse talent.

Outsource responsibilities.

Too small?

Amount of talent

Size of team

WHO IS ON YOUR TEAM?

Diversity of talent

Too bulky?

Let people go.

Reassign roles.

Work inside to fix it.

Talent? What talent?

A common problem with teams today is that they are too big. More heads do not necessarily make for more ideas or more output. On the contrary, the larger a team, the more difficult it is to coordinate, to motivate individuals within it, to manage.

What group size is optimal to perform most tasks? Usually from five to eight members. If your team is larger than that, you should have a good reason why— and a clear idea of the unique contribution each member makes.

When stuck, it becomes apparent that you might not have all the right team members to get out of the situation you're in. Selecting, retaining, and occasionally trimming members from the team is critical to your success as a leader. Too many members, and your team won't be able to work quickly. Too few, and it won't come up with good new solutions. A team with too many stray members—that is, a team that shares few common values— rarely gets to a workable consensus. Too many like-minded people, and the team will always get to the same predictable (read: boring) result. Do you need to alter your team's composition?

NEED TO RAISE THE STAKES? (PAGE 107) ▶
DO YOU SEE WHAT I SEE? (PAGE 140) ▶
NEED NEW BRAINPOWER? (PAGE 85) ▶

IDEA GUY/GAL

MOTIVATOR

ATTORNEY

FACILITATOR

PUBLIC RELATIONS

CONSULTANT

WRITER

ANALYST

MAINTENANCE ENGINEER

ARCHIVIST

TROUBLE SHOOTER

CEO

ACCOUNTANT

JACK OF ALL TRADES

PARTNER

COMPANY VETERAN

IT MANAGER

RESEARCHER

ENGINEER

PROCESS EXPERT

STAR PERFORMER

PAYROLL

RECRUITER

CULTURAL ICON

TRAINER

INVENTOR

NEW HIRE

INCULCATION EXPERT

CORPORATE FOLKLORIST

CFO

HR EXPERT

YOU

BELIEVER

COMMUNICATOR

OUTSIDER

QUALITY EXPERT

LAB MANAGER

RESEARCHER

MARKETER

NEGOTIATOR

Futurecast.

Sometimes teams get stuck because they don't see their next action as an incremental step on a journey to somewhere meaningful. One way to define what is meaningful is to "futurecast" (forecasting + imagination). Project out a few months, years, even decades to see a different view of the challenges ahead. Create competitors to test your battle worthiness. Examine how your industry intersects others. Witness how customers will change. Visualize it. Write it down. Then venture back to the present day. What will you now do differently based on the future you saw?

HOW DOES IBM FUTURECAST? (PAGE 121) ▶
DEDICATE SPACE FOR FUTURECASTING. (PAGE 100) ▶
SEE THE FUTURE? BUILD THE PROTOTYPE. (PAGE 115) ▶

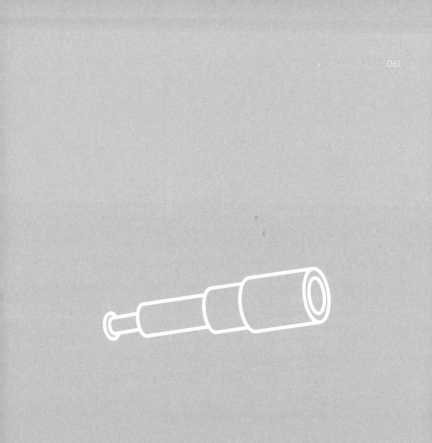

WHAT'S IN YOUR STARS? (PAGE 125) ▶

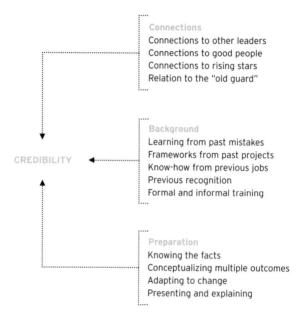

Connections
Connections to other leaders
Connections to good people
Connections to rising stars
Relation to the "old guard"

Background
Learning from past mistakes
Frameworks from past projects
Know-how from previous jobs
Previous recognition
Formal and informal training

CREDIBILITY

Preparation
Knowing the facts
Conceptualizing multiple outcomes
Adapting to change
Presenting and explaining

"I just have no cred."

Feel like you're not being heard? It may be because you lack credibility.

If you're looking to change this, we recommend "The Necessary Art of Persuasion" by Jay Conger. It's a great article about influence and credibility.

Credibility comes from two primary sources: your relationships and your experience. You may be stuck because you're a new leader of your team, or maybe because members don't think you're credible. If you find yourself stuck because you lack credibility, don't be shy about helping team members see your connections to other people they know and respect. This is not about name-dropping, but rather ensuring that you have a good working relationship with those who matter most to your team. Or, people may have heard of you, but don't know your skills. In this case, be certain to bring new fundamental insights, tools, or knowledge from your previous experience to the table to illuminate your value. Above all, be truthful about your skills. Cred is built on actions, not puffery.

NOT ALL POWER IS OFFICIAL. (PAGE 113) ▶
TOO MUCH POLITICS? (PAGE 109) ▶
NEED A LARGER NETWORK? (PAGE 136) ▶

OVERCOMING FEELING DIRECTIONLESS

Take-away: (1) Bring in provocative thinkers to challenge your own thinking. (2) Pick a topic valuable to all. (3) Work visually and rapidly. (4) Learn from everything that's said, wished, hoped for, and expressed.

How to stay relevant for future generations? That's the question the Japan Society faced on the eve of their 100th anniversary. For its first century, the group has promoted understanding and cooperation between Japan and the United States. What to do for their second 100 years on the planet? Perhaps rather than dictate that, it would be smarter to discover it. First, collaborate—in this case with The Japan Foundation Center for Global Partnership. Pick two provocative topics: Innovation and Community. Then hold retreats for visionaries across diverse fields to explore them. In doing so, new insights and perspectives come forward. A more systemic view of shared challenges and opportunities emerge. And ultimately, the Japan Society finds its powerful direction for a new era.

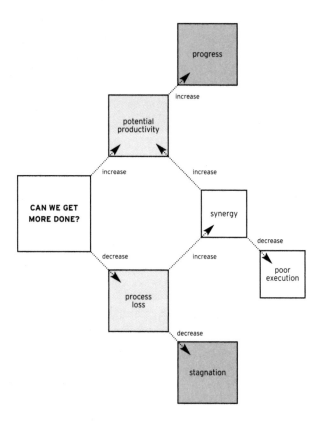

Why can't we get anything done?

Remember the answer to that old joke: "How do you get to Carnegie Hall? Practice, practice, practice." The same goes for teamwork. Coordination comes from practice. And, though it may be more mundane than the glamorous task of creating synergy, your skill in coordinating will determine your team's productivity more than anything else.

To learn more about these elements of team productivity, consult *Making the Team* by Leigh Thompson and *Group Process and Productivity* by Ivan Steiner.

Master this equation:

Team productivity =
** Potential productivity of the team**
− Process loss
+ Gains from working together (known
**   as the synergy factor)**

What can you control in your team's productivity equation? It may not be what you expect. Most leaders obsess about who gets on the team and their individual strengths. This is important, but not always the driver of results. Synergy is something leaders try to force (think about the team-building exercises you've attempted), but it's actually very difficult to engineer. Surprisingly, your greatest lever — minimizing process loss — often goes ignored. Focus on coordinating activity, clarifying roles, and ensuring efficient hand-offs — the areas in which you can make the largest impact.

SURROUNDED BY DRONES? (PAGE 71) ▶
RUNNING OUT OF TIME? (PAGE 152) ▶
NEED TO DELIVER THE TOUGH MESSAGE? (PAGE 131) ▶

All for one?
One for all?

Make sure you're measuring and rewarding the right behaviors. Steven Kerr's classic article, "On the Folly of Rewarding A While Hoping for B," discusses how to avoid the disconnect between what team members get rewarded for doing and what they know they should be doing to help the team or organization.

During its early years, DVD-rental giant Netflix got the metrics right. It reached one million subscribers faster than AOL had. Subscriber milestones were celebrated with companywide praise — the kind that took the entire team to Hawaii one year, for example.

Teams can become stuck because members are working at cross-purposes. When should people look out for themselves and when should they give more to the team? Effective teams are motivated through a combination of individual and team-based incentives.

If incentives are at the individual level, there is little reason to cooperate (think everyone working just for him or herself). If all the incentives are at the team level, there is little reason to contribute (think freeloaders in a tug-of-war). What is the right mix?

The balance between individual and team incentives should be in line with the amount of responsibility or control team members have over each area.

◀ ARE YOU MOTIVATING WITH HEART? (PAGE 55)
DO YOU ACKNOWLEDGE GREAT WORK OFTEN? (PAGE 111) ▶
READ MORE ABOUT INCENTIVES AT WWW.UNSTUCK.COM.

Teamwork is great, but only if you need it.

What's wrong with using a team, even if you don't need one? Plenty. Teamwork is both difficult and costly. Teams are only the right answer sometimes.

That said, if the morale or development benefits are big enough, deploying a team may make sense even when it isn't necessary. The point is to be deliberate when you form a team.

In the information age, teamwork has been billed as a panacea for productivity. Any time there is trouble in your team, the first question to ask is: Do we really need a team for this? Followed quickly by: OK, then how small can we make it? Some guidelines:

> If members are dependent on one another for different parts of the end product — a simplistic example is a factory assembly line — teamwork is necessary.

> If the task can benefit from social interaction and stimulation — for example, creativity or decision making — ditto.

> If there is a common group goal, assembling a team makes sense regardless of task.

> But in many other cases, especially those where one person has most of the skills required for a task, it doesn't make sense to rally a team.

ARE YOUR TEAM MEETINGS BALLISTIC? (PAGE 99) ▶
ARE THERE DIFFERENCES OF OPINION? (PAGE 140) ▶
WHO IS A QUIET ROCK STAR? (PAGE 139) ▶

DIFFERENCE: **DIVERSITY OF THOUGHT AND IDEAS**
LIKELY OUTCOME: **INNOVATION** (SEE PAGE 73)

SAMENESS: **UNIFORMITY AND STAGNANT THOUGHT**
CERTAIN OUTCOME: **GROUPTHINK** (SEE PAGE 72)

Groupthink.
Yep. Yep.

Irving Janis, author of *Groupthink*, studied and wrote about how group cohesion can erode the quality of decisions. How many times this week have you agreed to follow the will of your team, even though the direction wasn't the right one? As a leader your role is to ensure you can build team unity, not team conformity.

A group dominated by a thought leader performs no better than that leader working alone. In other words: Team cohesion is good, but groupthink isn't. A surprising number of individuals will change their views if the pull of the group is strong enough — even if they know from the get-go that the group is wrong. Individuals are always at risk of succumbing to this conformity — and the pull is even stronger in groups that have tight networks or are working on tasks where success is subjectively defined. Some tactics for avoiding groupthink:

> Make sure dissenting opinions get heard.

> Appoint an official devil's advocate.

> Challenge people to poke holes in the ideas that gain momentum.

> Remember, it is better to make changes while you still can than to roll out an idea that isn't thought through.

TAKE IT UP A NOTCH! (PAGE 107) ▶

WHAT'S REALLY IN YOUR TEAMMATES' BRAINS? (PAGE 140) ▶

WHERE DO YOU THINK BEST? (PAGE 100) ▶

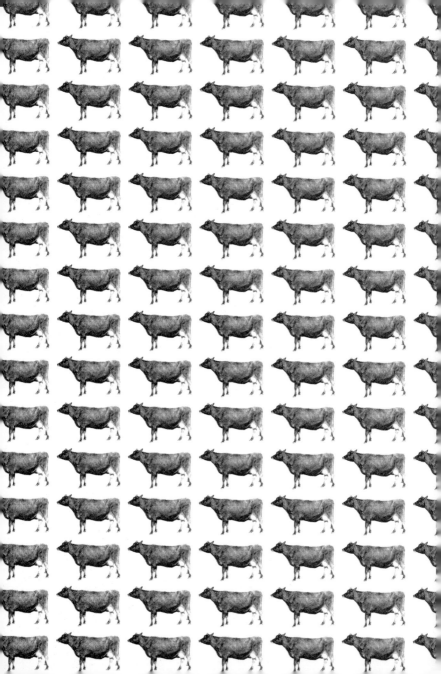

CASE STUDY: RETURNING TO YOUR ROOTS

How do you rescue a company in a complete tailspin? That's exactly the challenge Steve Jobs faced when he returned to **Apple** in 1997. Once a powerhouse in the world of personal computing, Apple had fallen far behind its competitors, prompting many to write them off as a "has-been." One of the first steps Jobs took as interim CEO was to return Apple to its roots of "insanely great" products. He terminated many projects and focused the company on the successful iMac, and the revolutionary iPod. His inspiring quest for greatness rekindled the sense of identity and pride that Apple employees once had. By concentrating on what Apple did best, Jobs returned the company not just to profitability but restored the passion for the brand among customers and employees alike.

OVERCOMING FEELING ALONE
Take-away: Sometimes getting unstuck requires going back to your roots.

Let your soul be your guide.

A team's soul — also known as its culture — reflects the implicit values and practices that prescribe acceptable behavior within it. That culture tells members how to fit in, how to succeed, how to contribute, and, likewise, how to get booted off the team if you don't fit in. Why is it important for team members to know their culture? Think about how out-of-place you feel when visiting a foreign country where you don't know the language or how things are done. Leaders can do a lot to shape the culture of their crew by simply expressing their own values and desires. But keep in mind that a team's culture — and the routines that support it — can emerge very quickly. The way things are done the first time, in the first meeting, before the first deadline, often gets institutionalized as "the way we do things around here." Be deliberate about every detail and symbol early on; they're vital to your success later.

Culture can be as powerful in shaping behavior as direct orders from a management team or compensation schemes. One CEO we work with recently said, "I may have huge power in my title, but the 150,000 people of this organization can render me powerless in the blink of an eye." That's because of culture. Researchers like Charles O'Reilly characterize cultures as social control systems, emphasizing the power of strong cultures and even comparing them to cults.

What are the informal rules that shape behavior on your team? Do they fully support your purpose and strategy?

◄ **WHAT DOES TRUST MEAN TO CULTURE?** (PAGE 52)
◄ **DOES YOUR CULTURE REFLECT YOUR PURPOSE?** (PAGE 51)
WHAT IS THE LANGUAGE OF YOUR CULTURE? (PAGE 118) ►

Give the movement a name.

A name builds identity while also promoting commitment and cohesion among teams. As Richard Hackman writes in *Groups That Work (And Those That Don't)*, escalation cycles—both positive and negative—abound in group dynamics. It's very important to keep an eye out—a system view—for the ripple effects of small symbols in your team.

For example: To dig Continental out of bankruptcy in 1994, Gordon Bethune was quick to name his turnaround strategy the "Go Forward Plan." He even developed clear names for each component: "Fund the Future," "Fly to Win," "Make Reliability a Reality," and "Working Together."

Names carry a story with them. One example: When IBM coined the term e-business, they were making a bold statement that all business would become electronic some day. And who better to help people move into that world than IBM? A name for your movement can help carry it from person to person, from stakeholder to stakeholder, like a piece of good gossip. What will you call your movement?

HOW STRAIGHTFORWARD IS YOUR NAME? (PAGE 86) ▶
◀ DOES YOUR NAME HAVE HEART? (PAGE 55)
CAN YOUR NETWORK SUPPORT THE MOVEMENT? (PAGE 136) ▶

NEVER LETTING A TEAM FEEL WORTHLESS

Take-aways: (1) To encourage new ways of working, reward new behaviors. (2) Explore new perspectives by collaborating in diverse teams made up of experts and non-experts. (3) Think broadly about entire systems to uncover hidden opportunities.

Year after year, GE consistently executes its way to strong growth. But to continue that trajectory, GE recently realized it had to nurture a culture that fuses flawless execution with breakthrough innovation. It's all about helping new behaviors emerge. Take, for example, GE Plastics—long focused on business customers. To innovate, they liberated themselves to think about everyday consumers. By thinking how GE's plastics technology could better serve businesses who in turn serve everyday people, the GE team was able to generate many radical new ideas. In the process, these teams learned new ways of working. And that's catalyzing the kind of innovative thinking that continues to keep GE at the top of its game.

Take over the TV station.

Make a list of every communication outlet you have at your disposal. Think about the mass-scale ones first, then more private venues (team meetings, for example). Above all: Don't limit your thinking to communication you pay for.

Then assess and prioritize your outlets: Which ones have reach? Which are under-utilized? Which are tired? Which could be combined to make your message more potent?

The moment a coup happens, revolutionaries take over the TV station. That is, they ensure they get air time to take their ideas to the masses. Move your team toward productive action by getting them to use the power of their communications—every ad, every speech, every retail outlet, every meeting, every press release, every customer meeting—as a chance to get your story out to the world.

ARE POLITICS AT PLAY? (PAGE 109) ▶
SPEAK CLEARLY (PAGE 86) ▶
HAVE THE TV STATION, BUT NEED THE NEWS? (PAGE 95) ▶

Put your idea down in words.

For many, the prospect of writing anything — let alone a well-crafted message — can be daunting. The good news? There are many time-tested tactics and strategies that can help. See page 172 for sources that can help you.

You can start by making some decisions up front about the final product: What should the reader take away? How should he or she feel after absorbing the message? What tone is appropriate — casual conversation or strict formality? What are the options for distributing your message: E-mail? On posters? In a speech? Get clear on the form, and the message will be easier to craft.

Great leaders place great importance on writing down their vision, their idea, their central driving purpose — and then sharing them with others. First articulations are difficult to create, but painfully necessary. Force yourself to pen a speech, a brochure, a film, or, if you must, a PowerPoint deck that helps you recount your team's vision. You'll immediately recognize your idea's vulnerability. Then rework its expression until it can fully withstand slings and arrows.

NEED A TIME AND PLACE TO CRAFT THE IDEA? (PAGE 92) ▶
WHAT'S THE HEADLINE? (PAGE 95) ▶
◀ CAN YOU GO OUTSIDE TO FORMULATE YOUR VISION? (PAGE 57)

Revive the team.
Bring in new brainiacs.

Think about what you're doing to keep each member of your team sharp. Research shows that American companies invest about 23.7 training hours per year, per person.

Are you ahead of or behind the curve?

If you view an organization as a living system, you come to understand that the population as a whole can be changed most quickly by deciding who exits that system, and, more important, who enters. Recruit. Recruit. Recruit. Often, a slight change in the composition of your team can make a radical difference in its ability to innovate. First, who should you ask to leave your team? Then, who should you recruit to bring a vital new perspective? Could even one new person give your team the lift it needs?

GIVE THE BRAINS ROOM TO WORK. (PAGE 100) ▶
HOW DOES IBM FIND TOP TALENT? (PAGE 121) ▶
SHARE YOUR CULTURE WITH THE BRAINIACS. (PAGE 123) ▶

Favor plainspeak over breathy bravado.

During his tenure leading GE, CEO Jack Welch advocated for straight-from-the-gut communication. To fight bureaucracy, honesty is vital.

When your team looks in the mirror, what does it see? Can you be brutally honest about what's going on? Now, can you find the courage and voice to get your point across in the most powerful fashion?

The pendulum is swinging back: Here's to the return of commonsense executives who, rather than leaning on breathy bravado, rely on honesty, a convincing vision of the future, and believable results. Make your team look in the mirror, then speak the truth. What's really going on that's holding it back? When is your next chance to communicate with your team — and how will you make it powerfully honest?

FAVOR PLAINSPEAK TO CLARIFY DECISIONS. (PAGE 157) ▶
◀ IS PLAINSPEAK A PART OF YOUR CULTURE? (PAGE 75)
ARE YOUR IDEAS BEING HEARD? (PAGE 112) ▶

Take-away: When pursuing your purpose, ask yourself, why exactly, do we do what we do? Dig deeper than your business strategy or your brand strategy to discover what truly motivates you and your team. What gets you out of the bed in the morning? What would the world miss if your organization were no longer there to provide it?

CASE STUDY: DISCOVERING YOUR PURPOSE

How can we reframe the values debate in modern American politics? That was the question The Center for American Progress (CAP), a new think-tank in Washington D.C. set out to answer. Founded in 2004 by John Podesta, former Chief of Staff in the Clinton administration, CAP was searching for language that would engage the heads—and hearts—of everyday Americans. The team soon realized that they could not find provocative language until they first articulated powerful ideas. Through the process of defining the vision and principles of today's Progressive movement, CAP sharpened their own purpose as an organization. CAP now uses the strategic framework they created to develop policy ideas, shape the dialogue of American politics, and keep the hope alive within their own organization.

Host a summit.

The Japan Society's effort to renew its strategy (detailed on page 65) offers a great illustration of the power of hosting a summit.

What would a summit for your team look like? Who could you invite — from both inside and outside your organization? How could you shake up people's thinking to bring in new ideas?

There are two approaches to strategy making. **Approach A:** Send a small team off, lock them in a room, then have them come back (usually with PowerPoint deck in hand) and convince everyone that they've discovered the right answer. **Approach B:** Invite a large swath of experts to a summit; skillfully use exercises, simulations, and mapping to forge a strategy; then when you disband, assign a dedicated team to execute it.

The benefit of using a summit to accomplish strategy making is that no one is as smart as everyone. That is, when brought together, great people can often come up with better thinking than they would have on their own. What's more, if the key stakeholders are part of the creation, there's no need for the laborious process of "selling" the strategy.

◄ HOW CAN YOU KICKSTART THE SUMMIT? (PAGE 60)
INVITE YOUR NETWORK TO THE SUMMIT. (PAGE 136) ►
GET TOPICS AND IDEAS AT WWW.UNSTUCK.COM.

CASE STUDY: GALVANIZING A MOVEMENT

There are more than 850,000 nonprofits in the United States—each with a sense of purpose. Environmentalism is the grandfather of the group, and arguably the world's largest cause. What are the origins of such a global movement? A passionate man with a vague cause by the name of **John Muir**. In 1892, Muir organized a small group of nature lovers "to make the mountains glad." Their name... simply The Sierra Club. For years the club remained directionless until, in 1901, its path became clear. Their preservationist vision grew to a national level after a battle over the proposed Hetch Hetchy Valley Dam in California. This single event crystallized Muir's direction and constituted one of the first movements for environmental protection.

OVERCOMING FEELING DIRECTIONLESS

Take-aways (1) A passion may seem directionless but can grow when challenged. (2) Be honest about values no matter how big you become.

Write a headline from the future.

Great leaders help people envision where their team's moonshot will take them. Write down a headline from the future. What will it say about all you have achieved? Now back it out: Step by step, how will you get there?

READY TO DELIVER ON THE VISION? (PAGE 102) ▶
◀ **DOES THE HEADLINE REFLECT YOUR PURPOSE?** (PAGE 51)
NEED A PROTOTYPE FIRST? (PAGE 115) ▶

HIT A WALL?

TRY
PAGE
47.

Process facilitator

Who keeps the team on track? How do you craft the flow of each exchange while maintaining focus and managing conflict?

Socio-emotional leader

Who is thinking about the heartbeat of each meeting? Who is tapped into team energy levels? Engagement?

CAN YOU SPLIT UP THE ROLES?

Recorder

Who captures literally every idea from the team? What system do you have to keep ideas specific, clear, and timely?

Devil's advocate

Who makes sure that you are considering all the angles and testing the logic? Warning: Too much devil can slow you down.

The meeting has gone ballistic.

Sometimes the process by which roles emerge on a team is organic. People just fall naturally into certain functions, whether or not it's the best thing for the team. When assigning roles to members of an existing group, be sure to recognize which already exist informally. Then either reassign or formalize these, as is most useful. Also, keep in mind it's usually a good idea to periodically rotate roles in order to share responsibilities.

Chaos is sometimes good. But when the group goes truly ballistic, it's important that certain players get assigned to formalized roles: The **process facilitator's** role requires 100 percent attention to the dynamics of people in the room (as opposed to the underlying content). The job is to defuse intense exchanges within the team, monitor time and participation, and keep things on track. The **socio-emotional leader's** role is to tend to morale, neutralize conflict, and keep the energy up. The **recorder's role** is to ensure that all meaningful dialogue is written down and documented; that way, all believe their thinking is being represented. And it is. The **devil's advocate** takes a countervailing view for the specific purpose of testing the logic of what's being said.

◄ WHAT'S THE INCENTIVE TO PLAY NICELY? (PAGE 68)
◄ IS A TEAM NECESSARY? (PAGE 69)
WHO ARE YOUR QUIET ROCK STARS? (PAGE 139) ►

Build a haven for radical thinking.

For toy giant Mattel, a haven for radical thinking means Project Platypus. In 2001 under the leadership of Senior VP Ivy Ross, team members were taken from all areas of Mattel (from finance to marketing) to work in an independent studio for three months at a time. The "platypi" experience was unique — a haven where Mattel could do some of its best thinking about new toy ideas and trends.

1. Get a room. Claim it.

2. Assemble a team of experts. Not just members of your stuck team, but outsiders as well.

3. Give each expert a key to the room.

4. Cover the walls with paper (or if you're flush with cash, whiteboards).

5. Now, visualize your strategy. (Diagram everything: purpose, strategy, competitive landscape, the facts, your coalition of partners, your message.)

6. Make this the room where you do your best thinking.

SHOW THE HAVEN TO THE WORLD. (PAGE 107) ▶
CAN THE THINKERS BE HEARD? (PAGE 112) ▶
◀ NOT RADICAL ENOUGH? FUTURECAST. (PAGE 60)

Deliver on your vision in 360°.

A visionary in 360°
customer service,
Hertz has forged many
firsts in the rental-car
industry —from the
first rental charge card
in 1926 to the first
in-car cellular phone
in 1988. To create the
Hertz #1 Club Gold
program, teams within
the company examined
the process of renting
a car, and came up
with ways to make
customers' lives easier
at every step. When
members arrive at
Hertz, their names
are displayed on an
up-to-the-minute
digital board, their
cars have been parked
close by under a
weather-protected
canopy — with the car
heaters running if it's
cold outside— and they
can drive away without
the hassle of signing a
rental agreement.

Once you have a purpose, it's important to enact it. Take the time to map out how your purpose translates into everything you do as a company. Think about each touch point: how you market, sell, please customers, strike partnerships, answer the phone. A map of that 360° experience is the first step in focusing a team on actions it can take.

◀ **DOES YOUR VISION MIRROR YOUR PURPOSE?** (PAGE 51)
KEEP YOUR LANGUAGE CONSISTENT. (PAGE 118) ▶
ACT FAST. THE CLOCK IS TICKING. (PAGE 152) ▶

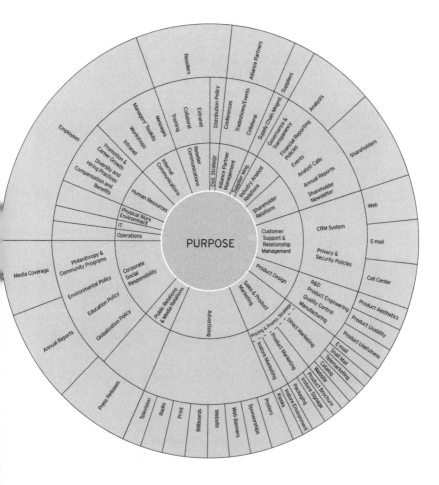

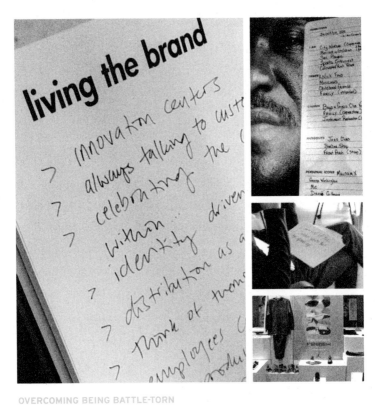

OVERCOMING BEING BATTLE-TORN

Take-away: Sometimes getting unstuck requires a new perspective—seeing the world through someone else's eyes. How does your customer truly see your company?

As a $400+ million division of Nike, Inc., the Brand Jordan team realized that its biggest competition did not reside outside the berm in Beaverton, but rather within its own group. The highly successful—but often battle-torn— team spent a lot of its time warring with itself. President Larry Miller decided to help his key leaders get unstuck by gathering them for a very unusual offsite meeting—in a hotel ballroom outfitted with a miniature city representing every Jordan product, ad, clothing line, and promotion. Instead of wearing hats from their day jobs, team members played the roles of specific customers. The group spent a full day in that miniature city, examining the Brand Jordan experience from the perspective of customers of all ages. In the process, the team came to understand how to close the gaps—in their offerings and also in how their team works together.

Commit to a world-stage event.

There is a tremendous value in declaring your purpose—and means of achieving it—in a massively public way. It is human nature to procrastinate. Without enactment, strategies remain exactly that—strategies, with no action to back them up. Avoid the problem: Commit to talking about your purpose (and the actions you're taking to deliver on it) on a world stage. Hold a customer briefing, analyst briefing, press briefing. It will kick your team into action. Fortunately, it's also human nature to perform, especially when your audience is waiting.

Every year eBay Inc. hosts eBay Live—a gathering of more than 10,000 of its most successful buyers and sellers. At this event, the company seeks input, announces major new features on eBay.com, and tests policies. The company sends 500 employees to the event. Leader Meg Whitman uses the event to bring clarity to strategy and to reconnect with the community that fuels her company.

◄ TAKE TO THE AIRWAVES. (PAGE 80)
◄ WHAT WILL BE THE NAME OF THE EVENT? (PAGE 77)
◄ WHAT WILL THE HEADLINES SAY? (PAGE 95)

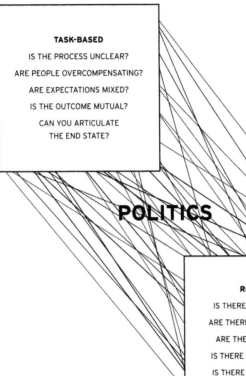

TASK-BASED

IS THE PROCESS UNCLEAR?

ARE PEOPLE OVERCOMPENSATING?

ARE EXPECTATIONS MIXED?

IS THE OUTCOME MUTUAL?

CAN YOU ARTICULATE
THE END STATE?

POLITICS

RELATIONAL

IS THERE DIRECT CONFLICT?

ARE THERE PRECONCEPTIONS?

ARE THERE STEREOTYPES?

IS THERE NO TEAM IDENTITY?

IS THERE A HIDDEN AGENDA?

IS THERE NO CONTEXT?

Politics.
Politics.
Politics.

Research by Karen Jehn delineates two different types of team conflict—relational and task-based—to show that the impact on team performance depends on the type of conflict. She found that a moderate amount of task-based conflict can actually improve performance, while relational conflict is usually detrimental.

It's obvious that politics are endemic to organizations. But what's sometimes less obvious is what kind of politics are at play. There are two fundamental types of politics: **relational** (people disagreeing on a personal level, where egos and hidden agendas rule) and **task-based** (people disagreeing about what work must be done, or how to do it). Which is at play in your team? What's the real basis of conflict? What are the stereotypes between groups (engineers versus marketers, for example) that may skew opinions? What are the blindnesses that prevent you from seeing the other camp's view? Now, make a list of what you can do this week to cut through the politics in your team.

NEED TO EMBRACE AN ENEMY? (PAGE 133) ▶
ARE YOU SURE WHERE PEOPLE STAND? (PAGE 140) ▶
WHAT IS UNOFFICIAL POWER? (PAGE 113) ▶

CASE STUDY: RECOGNIZING ALL ACHIEVEMENTS

Imagine if your business functioned like a national Olympic team—anything less than a medal would seem worthless. At the 1992 Barcelona Olympic Games, the **Spanish Olympic team** won an unprecedented 22 medals. At the time, many viewed the victory as a case of home court advantage (Spain had won only a handful of medals in the previous 100 years). When the Spanish took home 17 medals four years later in Atlanta, heads turned. How? The team made the decision to shift attention away from the one-time nature of the Olympics toward more frequent, smaller-scale competitions. The secret of the Spanish was to concentrate attention and resources on a constant system of metrics and performance-based rewards.

OVERCOMING FEELING WORTHLESS
Take-aways: (1) Create worth by making compensation and rewards more frequent and understood. (2) Think creatively about how to reward others.

Praise, praise, and more praise.

Gary VanSpronsen,
former Herman Miller
executive believes
that while praise is a
critical component of
performance, it's not
the only one. "Don't
mistake praise as a
surefire motivator—
it can sometimes have
the opposite result.
Rather, leaders often
inspire the greatest
performance through
engagement. Asking
an inquisitive question
can be a powerful
catalyst to get people
motivated. If you
find yourself giving
constant praise, mix
it up a bit. Instead,
ask a team member
what they're learning
on a project and what
they see as the next
steps. The question
will often lead to
conversations that
uncover new ways to
increase performance
of the team."

Appreciation. Respect. Acknowledgment. Encouragement. More than compensation or promotion, these forms of public recognition can motivate and inspire individuals to give their all to their team. Offering praise (or punishment) in public heightens the impact of its delivery. It also acts as a strong signal to onlookers as to what is important and consequential in the group. To be meaningful, praise must be discerning and consistent. Only offer praise when it is warranted—but always offer it then. And remember, the more public, the better.

◄ LEAVE NO ROOM FOR MISUNDERSTANDING. (PAGE 86)
CONSIDER THE "HAVES" AND "HAVE-NOTS." (PAGE 127) ►
◄ NEED A PERFECT VENUE? (PAGE 92)

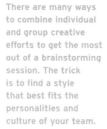
Before any idea can become brilliant, it must first be heard.

There are many ways to combine individual and group creative efforts to get the most out of a brainstorming session. The trick is to find a style that best fits the personalities and culture of your team.

Is it better to have members spend time before a meeting writing down their own ideas — and then launch the brainstorm with each person reporting individually? Or is your team so comfortable with e-mail that the best collaboration is going to arise out of an electronic sharing of ideas — in real time, or sequentially?

Group dynamics can easily prevent that. Is your team at a standstill because the person who has the idea to get you unstuck is never heard? Can you find a way to improve the way your team shares its ideas? Recent research shows that spontaneous, on-your-feet brainstorming is rarely the best method of generating ideas. A serial approach often works better. Gather the team for a discussion of the problem and let people work together for a while, then on their own. Force people to write down their ideas and share them in writing. Writing induces clarity. Clarity induces action. The trick here is to find the right rhythm of teamwork and working as individuals. What is the meter of your team when it's working at its best?

◄ CAN'T HEAR IDEAS OVER THE ARGUMENTS? (PAGE 99)
◄ HAVE NO "CRED" TO SHARE YOUR IDEA? (PAGE 63)
NEED TO GET PEOPLE REALLY LISTENING? (PAGE 147) ►

Go where the unofficial power lies.

Karen Stephenson has studied networked systems for decades. As demonstrated by her research, to understand how an organization works, you need to map all the different networks within the company: the formal network of people based on titles and rank, the informal network of players who get the work done, the network of people who function as hubs to connect teams.

Literally mapping these networks will teach you who to win over to your cause, and who may be getting excluded.

There are people who live at the top of the organizational chart, and there are those who wield power regardless of rank. You need to rally both — but especially the latter. These team members are often the first critical allies for your cause. They can support your purpose and also your path to achieving it. But don't just try to inculcate them into your cause. Give them the tools to take your story to a wider audience of supporters. Provide clear language to tell the story, back it up with logic, and make yourself accessible for any questions or ideas down the road.

MAP WHERE THE UNOFFICIAL POWER LIES. (PAGE 140) ▶
WHO STANDS IN YOUR WAY? (PAGE 133) ▶
◀ WILL YOU APPEAL TO HEART OR INTELLECT? (PAGE 55)

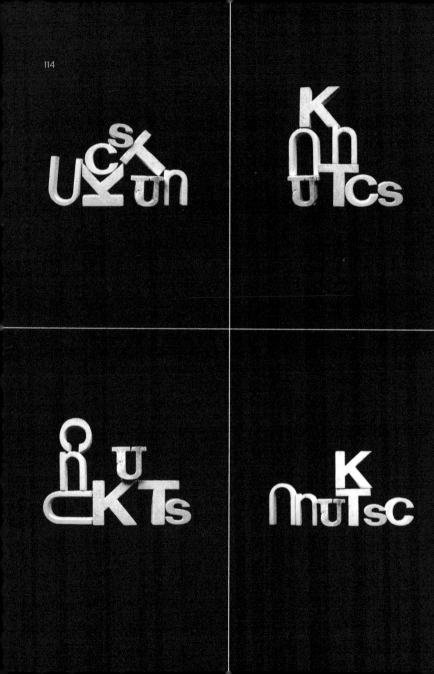

Invent a prototype of the end state.

In addition to helping clarify the end goal, creating a prototype can also facilitate innovation in developing the goal. IDEO, a successful product development firm, uses this method not just to visualize the end state but to actually stimulate new ideas about what that goal may look like.

What is the earliest stage in your process that you can start making a prototype? Can you take action today?

Teams get stuck because they simply can't see the end state—and no one knows which steps to take without knowing the destination. Rather than spend all your time debating about where your journey will lead, form a prototype of the destination. Draw it out. Make a scenario. Create a room that literally shows the journey a customer will take with your company over time. Once you have developed a prototype, your conversations will be more on point.

◀ **NEED NEW BRAINPOWER?** (PAGE 85)
WHAT'S YOUR CURRENT "MODE?" (PAGE 153) ▶
BUILD A LIVING LAB. (PAGE 128) ▶

Control the language.
Control the debate.

While at Sun Microsystems, Dr. Paul Pangaro created a program whose intent is to expand the language of conversations between software developers and the company. The idea is that conversation is delimited by language.

Only by constantly broadening language can Sun continuously regenerate partnerships with software developers. Pangaro calls such processes co-evolutionary, because they are symbiotic, adaptive, and assure maximum productivity.

Words frame thoughts. Thoughts express connections. Connections enable people to tell themselves stories about what the cause stands for. One way to get unstuck is to get your team to concentrate on choosing the right words to tell your story to the world. Encourage it to coin a term for what you do. Invent a new category if it gives you permission to tell the story to your advantage. Own the vocabulary that's used to describe the industry. What's more, in opening up the language you use, you actually increase your chances of uncovering new opportunities or seeing a situation in a new light.

◀ WHAT DO YOU STRESS IN YOUR LANGUAGE? (PAGE 55)
DOES LANGUAGE LEAD TO YOUR NORTH STAR? (PAGE 125) ▶
FOR IBM, NEW TALENT CREATES NEW LANGUAGE. (PAGE 121) ▶

▷ DOES YOUR TEAM HAVE ITS OWN VOCABULARY? THINK ABOUT
THE WORDS YOU USE DAILY THAT ARE SPECIFIC TO YOUR TEAM.
JOT A FEW OF THESE WORDS BELOW . . .

WHICH OF THESE WORDS ARE TIRED? WHICH ARE JARGON? HOW CAN
YOU FOCUS THE LANGUAGE TO ATTACK THE PROBLEM AT HAND?

Take-away: Sometimes actions speak louder than words. Put people in a simulation to convey your point.

In the late 1990s, IBM had two big challenges: finding great talent (dot-coms were winning the best Ph.D. researchers) and positioning itself as an Internet leader. CEO Lou Gerstner, instead of feeling overwhelmed, took on both challenges simultaneously with an event named Summer Jam—a worldwide jam session held concurrently in seven IBM labs. It paired the company's best researchers with 1,200 Ph.D. summer hires. The topic of the day? The future of computing. The event's centerpiece was a three-hour simulation that pitted teams against one another to develop the most meaningful solution for customers circa 2020. The teams had to aggregate technologies, seek funding from venture capitalists, pitch their ideas, and rapidly evolve their solutions based on feedback. The result? IBM increased the percentage of summer hires who signed on permanently; all saw the power in IBM.

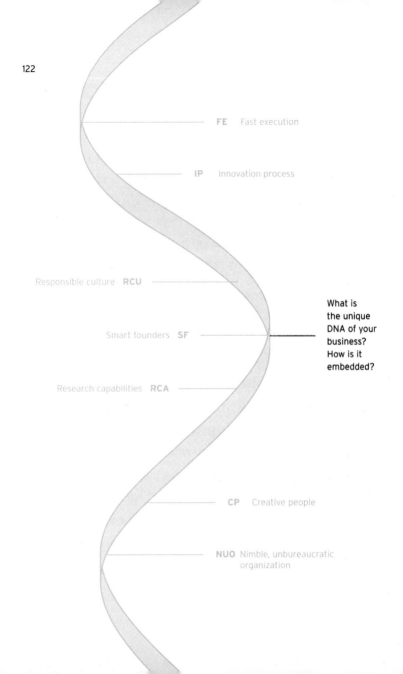

FE Fast execution

IP Innovation process

Responsible culture RCU

Smart founders SF

Research capabilities RCA

What is
the unique
DNA of your
business?
How is it
embedded?

CP Creative people

NUO Nimble, unbureaucratic
organization

Make every cell the holder of the genetic code.

As record stores struggle to survive, independent California chain Amoeba Records has remained the clear exception to the rule. The centerpiece to Amoeba's success is a team—ranging from semipro musicians to producers and DJs—that lives and breathes music. This love of music is the unique DNA that makes up each Amoeba cell.

Everyone must be a keeper of the vision—responsible for delivering on your purpose. Meet. Talk. Publish your vision for everyone to read. Create symbols and stories within your company culture that remind people of what you're doing—and why. Don't leave out a single person.

◀ DON'T MISTAKE GENETICS FOR GROUPTHINK. (PAGE 71)
◀ WHEN YOU HAVE THE CODE, HOW DO YOU SHARE IT? (PAGE 92)
◀ DO YOU HAVE THE RIGHT PEOPLE TO BEGIN WITH? (PAGE 57)

Take the time to chart a path to your North Star.

We believe that every organization has a North Star—a guiding purpose that remains true over time. Often, the trick is finding that North Star through all the haze. First, take the time to locate, describe, and define it. Then help others see that North Star—only then can your team navigate by it. Write that purpose down. Literally create a document, a scroll, a poster, an entire room that explains your North Star—and how you intend to use it to influence how you get from here (a moment of being stuck) to there (success).

◀ READY TO BUILD A PROTOTYPE OF WHAT YOU SEE? (PAGE 115) ▶
HOW LONG UNTIL YOU GET THERE? (PAGE 152) ▶
BEFORE SETTING OFF, CONSIDER YOUR "MODE." (PAGE 153) ▶

CASE STUDY: LEADING WITH RESOLVE

Few conflicts rival the tension of the **Cuban missile crisis**: communication breakdowns, grave consequences, and clearly opposing forces. Despite each day of mounting drama, the role of leadership, communication, and "calm determinism" (to use Kennedy's own words) proved essential to resolving the impasse. The Kennedy-Khrushchev pact that marked the end to the crisis should be a reassurance to all battle-torn leaders that in every conflict there is room for compromise and progress.

EASING TENSION OF A BATTLE-TORN TEAM
Take-aways: (1) Without open communication, there is limited hope of moving forward. (2) Remember your wider network and embrace it when you need it most. (3) Set a timeline to resolve issues.

Haves. Have-nots.

Groups exalt certain traits, and each group
exalts different ones. Gender. Marital status.
Education. Ethnicity. Title. Functional area.
Tenure. Credentials. All can be distinguishing
factors, and each comes with a label. It's
common for a group to elevate the haves
(those who possess the desired traits)
above the have-nots (those who don't).
Sometimes—whether blatantly or subtly—
a group attaches such strong stereotypes
to the haves and the have-nots that the
team members cannot do productive work
together. (Classic examples: engineering
versus marketing, men versus women, old-
time employees versus new hires.) What can
you do to restore unity to a fractured team?

Remind them of their team identity.

Publicly reject the stereotypes that divide
the team. Point out exceptions to them.

Change the composition of the group to
create balance, rather than token diversity.

◄ **HOW DIFFERENT IS PEOPLE'S THINKING?** (PAGE 71)
WHERE DO PEOPLE STAND? (PAGE 140) ►
◄ **ARE MEETINGS GOING BALLISTIC?** (PAGE 99)

Build a living lab.

A "living lab" is a prototype that presents opportunities to test out your best thinking. You can create living labs for new products by building a physical room where you house all parts of the solution so that consumers can come try them out. But don't limit yourself to that. You can also build living labs for less concrete things such as partnership models. Technology leader Hewlett-Packard recently built a living lab in a rural Indian village to fight poverty, increase literacy, and generate jobs—while learning more about how to effectively conduct business in that region and to form new kinds of partnerships along the way.

Living labs can be helpful in convincing a skeptical audience of a new vision. Mercedes-Benz U.S.A. CEO Michael Jackson's vision was to keep its customers for life. To reach this goal, Jackson needed to convince dealers to postpone high margins for new services, new systems, and a technology infrastructure. Instead of pitching the idea to his dealers, Jackson invited them to experience it. At the annual sales meeting, he built a 10,000-square-foot dealership of the future—a place where every element worked to increase customer loyalty. The result? Jackson gathered the support he needed to push forward.

◀ **HAVE THE LAB, BUT NO IDEAS?** (PAGE 60)
◀ **HAVE THE IDEAS? TAKE TO THE AIRWAVES.** (PAGE 80)
◀ **ARE YOU BEING TOO CONFORMIST?** (PAGE 72)

**COMPANY
CULTURE**

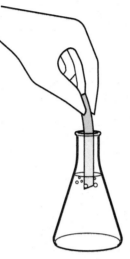

STABLE   **VOLATILE**

All elements
aligned to
deliver on
the vision

Unfocused;
political;
chock-full of
free radicals

The tough message

Laying the groundwork:
Why is the topic a top priority?
What are the trade-offs?
Why isn't there a silver bullet?
Why has decision making been difficult?

Reaching a decision:
What is the reasoning?
What is the decision?
What are the intended consequences?
What is the timeline for action?

Phrases to avoid:

"My way or the highway . . ."

"My facts say . . ."

"I don't have time to explain . . ."

Deliver the tough message.

Keep criticism constructive. Consider the words of William McKnight, an early chairman of 3M: "Management that is destructively critical when mistakes are made kills initiative. And it's essential that we have many people with initiative if we are to continue to grow." 3M has grown indeed—from making sandpaper (McKnight's days) into the $16 billion giant it is today.

Is something that's gone unspoken keeping the team back? Is there an unacknowledged rift separating the group? What about a performance issue that needs to be dealt with so members don't think a team member is loafing? Has one member wronged another? Perhaps it's time to deliver a tough message— take someone out of a post, put two warring factions in a room and work out differences, encourage someone to step up to a higher level of performance.

◄ FIRST, SPEAK CLEARLY. (PAGE 86)
◄ SECOND, BE HONEST. (PAGE 52)
THIRD, DON'T WAIT TOO LONG . . . (PAGE 157) ►

WANTED

GODZILLA

HEIGHT: 400 feet
WEIGHT: 1,000 tons
CRIME: Stomping ideas
LAST SEEN: Pages 50–64

Embrace thine enemy.

Another tactic is to get factions within the company to focus their venom outside of the company, toward the real competition. Choosing an outside enemy can bring your internal team closer together. A common enemy, or another external threat, unites a team.

Who are the outside competitors that truly irk your team? Which would you be the most proud to beat? Now, rally your team around defeating them.

Is your team stuck because there is an "enemy" in the organization trying to defeat the acceptance of your idea or your approach? Make a list of the people who stand against you and then:

1. Befriend them.

2. Convince them.

3. Get into a true dialogue that can improve your idea.

4. Invite them in.

5. Have them headhunted into a different company.

HOW WILL PEOPLE RESPOND? (PAGE 140) ▶

◀ **CONTROL THE LANGUAGE.** (PAGE 118)

DON'T FORGET YOUR NETWORK. (PAGE 136) ▶

The RAZR team was given a clear challenge, a very real deadline, and permission to break any rules that got in their way.

OVERCOMING FEELING EXHAUSTED
Take-aways: (1) Shake things up. (2) Don't be afraid to break the rules. (3) Craft a compelling story to inspire your teams.

How do you revive a once-great company that has lost its way? Motorola practically invented the cell phone and at one point controlled roughly 40 percent of the wireless-telephone market. But by 2003, fast-rising Nokia had taken over Motorola's #1. What's more, inside Motorola people were growing demoralized, tired, and unsure of how to break out of the doldrums. They needed a spark. And they found it when they assembled a team of their best engineers and designers to invent the next-generation mobile phone. They were given a clear challenge, a very real deadline, and permission to break any rules that got in the way of their breakthrough thinking. The result—the wildly popular ultra-thin RAZR cell phone. Motorola was back in the game. The company not only created a revolutionary product, it also re-energized the brand and gave employees a reason to again be proud.

Strong network.
Weak network.

The notion that weak bonds may at times be more helpful than strong bonds can be counterintuitive. Wouldn't a strong relationship always be better than a weak one? Not when you consider the pressure to conform and how decisions may be compromised if people have to worry about how a decision will affect their relationships.

Mark Granovetter's article "The Strength of Weak Ties" offers a great discussion of how important it is to incorporate a mix of strong and weak bonds into networks.

Bonds connect people within a network. Strong network bonds pull people together, while weak bonds serve as a doorway to a new group, new team, or new talent pool. (Think of a new person you've just met who then introduces you to her set of experts.) To be effective, your team needs to have the right mix of strong bonds and weak bonds between members—and access to the right resources outside the team. The bonds within the group can help you and the team. If you need a team that has a close, intimate feel, ensure that you have more strong bonds than weak. If diversity of thought is critically important, ensure that you have more weak bonds.

◄ **REACH OUT TO THE WEAK NETWORK.** (PAGE 85)
◄ **WHERE'S THE UNOFFICIAL POWER IN THE NETWORK?** (PAGE 113)
WHAT DOES EVERYONE IN THE NETWORK THINK? (PAGE 140) ►

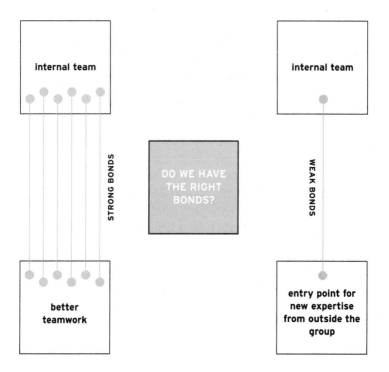

[Insert your rock star here.]

Find the quiet rock star.

The tendency for many managers is to try to change the communication style of the quiet rock star. It's better to have everyone speaking up to make themselves heard, right?

While this may work in theory, the fact is that communication styles are difficult to change. They are often formed in childhood and reinforced over time. What is your communication style? When are you likely to be overlooked?

Be sure to listen carefully — especially to the quiet rock stars of the group. Those with great talent who avoid taking center stage: The woman on your team who constantly handicaps her own ideas, the foreign-born manager who avoids eye contact, the first-year associate who sits quietly rather than getting involved in the debate. These are all people who may possess the next big idea. You just have to get it out of them.

◄ CAN THE ROCK STAR BE HEARD? (PAGE 112)
◄ HOW DO YOU MOTIVATE ROCK STARS? (PAGE 68)
◄ IS RESPECT FOR EVERY VOICE A PART OF YOUR SOUL? (PAGE 75)

Create a mind map to see the differences in people's views.

One of the quickest ways to find an approach for getting unstuck is to map the problem at hand (or, for that matter, the strategy for solving that problem). The purpose of a mind map is to show the key ideas and elements of any given idea, problem, or solution—and how they relate to each other. So, take a pen in hand and begin to diagram. Along the way, ask others to draw relationships they see in their heads. This technique is a rapid way to see the differences in views and to hammer out a collective vision that's more powerful than any one individual's mind map. From there, use the map to help share the thinking with others.

◄ **NEED SOMETHING TO MAP? MAP A PROTOTYPE.** (PAGE 115)
◄ **NEED NEW THINKING?** (PAGE 85)
◄ **SEE ANY OUTSTANDING PLAYERS IN YOUR MAP?** (PAGE 111)

Use this key to start your map.

⊙	IDEA
⊙	PERSON
ⓘ	ISSUE
⊙	CONNECTION

CASE STUDY: KEEPING COOL UNDER PRESSURE

The story of **Apollo 13** is legendary. The struggle of James Lovell, John Swigert, and Fred Haise will forever be told by people of all ages. No degree of detail, however, can replicate the intensity of the problems faced by NASA in April 1970. The rupture of oxygen tank No.2 created a "stuck" of astronomical proportion. The pressure to keep the crew alive (more than 200,000 miles from Earth) was intensified by the worldwide scrutiny of millions of TV viewers. The entire NASA team worked day and night to craft a safe re-entry, including fashioning a makeshift CO_2 filter using only the contents of the ship. NASA and the mission's astronauts had every opportunity to be overwhelmed, but kept their cool.

OVERCOMING FEELING OVERWHELMED
Take-aways: (1) Remember the people who depend on you most. (2) Don't permit scrutiny to dull your edge. (3) Surround yourself with every resource to get the job done.

Start with the control points of the system.

How can you identify the control points in your team's system? First, start with the symptoms you are observing. What is their most immediate cause? And what does that relate to? Trace the relationships and focus on the hubs.

And don't worry too much about everything else. As we've said, great leaders are systems thinkers: They can visualize the entire system that needs to change, then make pinpoint changes within that system to maximize the performance of the whole. What's more, they don't concern themselves with all the other noise in the system—they sponsor and drive specific initiatives at the points of control and leave the rest for natural evolution.

◀ REMEMBER THE UNOFFICIAL NETWORK. (PAGE 113)
◀ CAN YOU COMMUNICATE THE CONTROL POINTS? (PAGE 86)
TRY EXERCISES ON SYSTEMS THINKING AT WWW.UNSTUCK.COM.

Startle people.

"...Sony United is like an airplane.... The cabin class is united. The business class is getting united. It's the first class that I have the biggest problem with..."

— Sir Howard Stringer, CEO, Sony Corporation

OVERCOMING FEELING ALONE
Take-aways: (1) Make sure you have a culture that is based on the same philosophy as your products. (2) Don't be afraid to buck tradition. (3) A common goal brings a culture together.

In 2005, Sony was riding a five-year decline in its shareholder value. While its early success had been the result of product divisions operating independently of each other, this was a carryover from the analog world. As digital media emerged, products had to be able to talk to each other. And Sony found that for this to happen, the people inside the company had to learn to talk to each other as well. Sony's board named Howard Stringer to be CEO—the first non-Japanese to hold the post. His goal— flatten hierarchies, give younger people more prominent leadership roles, and get closer to customers. By uniting the different product divisions, all employees can come together with the common goal of returning the company to greatness.

▷ HOW DO PEOPLE EXPERIENCE THE PURPOSE BEHIND YOUR BRAND? IS IT
EXPLICIT? CHOOSE THREE EXAMPLES (HOWEVER SPECIFIC). ELABORATE.

EXAMPLE ONE

EXAMPLE TWO

EXAMPLE THREE

COMPARE EACH EXAMPLE TO THE DIAGRAM ON PAGE 103.
IS YOUR PURPOSE CLEAR TO THE PEOPLE THAT MATTER MOST?

Make your brand a manifestation of your company's purpose.

An authentic brand can often increase momentum (something that can give the team the bravery to get going again when they've had a setback). The most authentic brands are those where there is no gap between the purpose of the company and its actions, no gap between what it aspires to be and how it acts every day. (Think Nike, eBay, Sony, Disney.) Make your brand a one-to-one match with the purpose of your company.

◀ **DOES YOUR TEAM UNDERSTAND ITS PURPOSE?** (PAGE 123)
◀ **HOW WILL YOUR BRAND BE PERCEIVED IN 3 YEARS?** (PAGE 60)
VISIT WWW.UNSTUCK.COM TO BUILD A STATEMENT OF PURPOSE.

Tick. Tick. Tick.

Crunches can have both beneficial and detrimental effects on team productivity. One of the team processes that is most vulnerable to collapse under time pressure is brainstorming.

You can rush to a brainstorm meeting, and race out to tackle a million things when it's over. But you need to set up — and religiously guard — a designated time for collaborative creativity to occur. Just 20 minutes can make a big difference — as long as people know that they get the whole time and that it's enough time to make some progress.

Teams tend to optimize for everything except time. That is, they want to optimize how much data they collect, how they use resources, how many people they involve. But they often fail to take time into account. The skillful use of time can give you a great advantage over your competitors. Companies that measure results compared with the time invested tend to outperform their peers. All of which is a long-winded way of saying, get going. Deploy. Learn. And then course correct.

◀ **IS TIME THE BANE OF YOUR EXISTENCE?** (PAGE 145)

◀ **WANT TO SPEED UP THE CLOCK?** (PAGE 107)

NOT SURE ABOUT A DECISION? (PAGE 157) ▶

Be clear about which mode you are in.

How does your company move from one mode to another? Is it typically a strategic decision? Or is it a reaction? If you find yourself more reactionary, it might be worth visiting page 51.

Change requires two modes: blue-sky mode ("Given a clean slate, what would we do to live out our vision?") and tuning mode ("Given the hand we've been dealt, how should we proceed?"). Often, standstills in groups result from the blue-sky people being dragged down by the tuning-mode people, or the tuning-mode people thinking the blue-sky people are nuts. This issue can be solved by declaring which mode you're in — and ensuring everyone else is in that same mode. At the next meeting you go to, observe who is in which mode. You might be surprised.

◄ AFTER THE MEETING, DECLARE YOUR MODE. (PAGE 80)
◄ LOOKING FOR A FUTURE MODE? (PAGE 60)
◄ ARE YOUR MODES TOO COMPLEX? (PAGE 86)

[IT COULD BE WORSE.]

In June 1962, **Alcatraz** prisoners Frank Morris and brothers John and Clarence Anglin made a break for it. Although serious doubt exists about the success of the escape, the jailbreak remains the only "unresolved" case in the history of The Rock. The escape plan involved handmade drills, guard uniforms, and imitation human heads to deter nighttime guards. The men took to the water using raincoats as crude life vests and a makeshift raft. The police investigation turned up all the tools of the escape, but no sign of these three men.

OVERCOMING FEELING HOPELESS
Take-aways: (1) Desperate times may require desperate measures. (2) Be methodical. Be sequential. Every gain is a step in the right direction. (3) Stay out of jail.

Decide.

Are you absolutely
stuck between one
decision and another?
Have you thought
about every possible
outcome and can't
find a clear winner?

Step 1:
Choose heads or tails.

Step 2:
Resolve yourself to
the outcome.

Step 3:
Turn to page 153.

Step 4: Did the result
of the toss make
you think differently
about the decision?
Would you honor
your commitment to
the coin toss? Why?
Why not?

A decision today is often twice as worthy as a decision tomorrow. There is a deep opportunity cost of not deciding. This, though widely known, is rarely considered. Whether it's because you have not enough or too much data, are tortured by potential political backlash, don't know that a decision is required, or are simply afraid of losing your job, keep in mind that not deciding is likely to perpetuate a state of being stuck. This, more than anything else, is what will be most damaging. So, if we have one piece of advice, it would be: Close this book—and go make that decision.

◄ **REACHED A TOUGH DECISION?** (PAGE 131)
◄ **DON'T LOSE SIGHT OF THE NORTH STAR.** (PAGE 125)
◄ **EXCITED ABOUT THE DECISION? GIVE IT A NAME.** (PAGE 77)

TRY IT AGAIN — THIS TIME WITH MORE BRAVERY.

Whether you're responsible for yourself, a team, a division, or an entire company, thinking about the whole system is vital. Take a moment to get a pen and annotate the diagram to the right. What still needs fixing in your system? Which exercises in this book did you do, and which others must you now undertake? Look at the paths we suggest on page 162 for direction and inspiration. Reconsider your system in the context of the Serious Seven (page 28). Take a second pass through the book to find new ideas and actions to try. The second time around, be fearless. And be careful what you wish for.

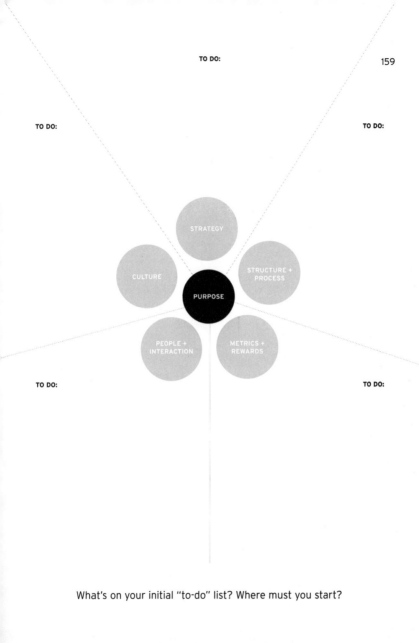

TO DO:

TO DO:

TO DO:

STRATEGY

STRUCTURE + PROCESS

CULTURE

PURPOSE

PEOPLE + INTERACTION

METRICS + REWARDS

TO DO:

TO DO:

What's on your initial "to-do" list? Where must you start?

DIGGING DEEPER.

PATHS TO TRY.

We hope you've taken your own path through this book, moving from exercise to exercise based on progress and your intuition about what will work best. That said, we think a more structured road map may also be useful. The paths below, organized by which of the Serious Seven best describes your predicament, offer another way to navigate the book or help you retrace steps that were particularly useful.

Overwhelmed

NOTES: PATHS THAT WORKED FOR ME.

Record the paths you took through UNSTUCK. Which tools made an impact? In what order? Who else on your team should now go on the journey you did?

SOURCES.

Throughout this book, where possible, we've tried to bake in the insight, theory, data, and work of great thinkers—so that you don't have to know the theory to get the result. That said, now that you're learning to get unstuck, you might want to do some additional reading on the topics and methods in this book. Here's a list of readings that we used as sources and think are worth your time.

PAGE 21 David A. Nadler and Michael Tushman, "A Congruence Model for Organizational Effectiveness," *Organizational Assessment: Perspectives on the Measurement of Organizational Behavior and the Quality of Work Life* (New York: John Wiley and Sons, 1980).

PAGE 51 Frank LaFasto and Carl E. Larson, *When Teams Work Best* (Thousand Oaks, CA: Sage, 2001).

PAGE 52 Vanessa Druskat and Steven Wolff, "Building the Emotional Intelligence of Groups," *Harvard Business Review*, March 2001.

PAGE 63 Jay A. Conger, "The Necessary Art of Persuasion," *Harvard Business Review*, June 1998.

PAGE 67 Leigh Thompson, *Making the Team* (New Jersey: Prentice Hall, 1999).

PAGE 67 Ivan Steiner, *Group Process and Productivity* (New York: Academic Press, 1972).

PAGE 68 Steven Kerr, "On the Folly of Rewarding A While Hoping for B," *Academy of Management Executive*, vol. 9, 1995.

PAGE 71 Irving Janis, *Groupthink; Psychological Studies of Policy Decisions and Fiascoes* (Boston: Houghton Mifflin, 1982).

PAGE 75 Charles O'Reilly, "Corporations, Culture, and Commitment," *California Management Review*, vol. 31(4), 1989.

PAGE 77 J. Richard Hackman, ed., *Groups That Work (And Those That Don't)*, (San Francisco: Jossey-Bass, 1990).

PAGE 77 Brian O'Reilly, "The Mechanic Who Fixed Continental," *FORTUNE*, December 1999.

PAGE 83 Mary Munter, *Guide to Managerial Communication* (New York: Prentice Hall, 2002).

PAGE 85 Chris Thompson, Eustace Koon, William H. Woodwell Jr., Julie Beauvais, "Training for the Next Economy: An ASTD Industry Report on Trends in Employer-Provided Training in the United States," American Society for Training & Development, 2002.

PAGE 86 Jack Welch, *Jack: Straight from the Gut* (New York: Warner Books, 2001).

PAGE 95 Copyright *The San Francisco Chronicle*. Reprinted by permission.

PAGE 100 Chuck Salter, "Ivy Ross Is Not Playing Around," *Fast Company*, November 2002.

PAGE 109 Karen Jehn, "A Multimethod Examination of the Benefits and Detriments of Intragroup Conflict," *Administrative Science Quarterly 40*, 1995.

PAGE 113 Karen Stephenson, "Diversity: A Managerial Paradox," *Clinical Sociology Review*, 1994.

PAGE 121 Steve Lohr, "I.B.M. Opens the Doors of Its Research Labs to Surprising Results," *New York Times*, July, 13, 1998.

PAGE 123 Bill Breen, "What's Selling in America: Part 1 of 5. Amoeba Music Marches to Its Own Beat," *Fast Company*, January 2003.

PAGE 127 Mercer Human Resource Consulting, People at Work Survey (2002). As printed in "Outsourcing: Success Steps to Observe for Your Company," *HR Focus*, September 2003.

PAGE 128 Debra Dunn and Keith Yamashita, "Microcapitalism and the Megacorporation," *Harvard Business Review*, August 2003.

PAGE 134 Adam Lashinsky, "RAZR'S Edge: How a Team of Engineers and Designers Defied Motorola's Own Rules to Create the Cellphone that Revived Their Company," *FORTUNE*, June 1, 2006.

PAGE 136 Mark Granovetter, "The Strength of Weak Ties: A Network Theory Revisited," *American Journal of Sociology*, vol. 78(6), 1983.

PAGE 149 Marc Gunther, "The Welshman, the Walkman, and the salarymen," *FORTUNE*, June 1, 2006.

PAGE 151 John Peterman, "The Rise and Fall of the J. Peterman Co.," *Harvard Business Review*, September 1999.

Looking for more ideas
on getting unstuck?

Visit www.unstuck.com

for tools, techniques,
and information you can put into practice.

BE KIND. NOW THAT YOU'RE UNSTUCK, HELP SOMEONE ELSE.

If you know someone (or an entire team for that matter) who is stuck, do them the favor of passing on this book. Or if you're feeling particularly philanthropic, buy each of them a copy of this book.

THANK YOUS.

Before we sign off, we should thank a few people. First, a thank you to Adrian Zackheim and Janet Goldstein at Portfolio and Viking Penguin, respectively, for their willingness to take a gamble on us. We are also grateful to the leaders, students, and friends who read drafts through this process, tested the tools, and provided valuable feedback.

Keith would like to thank: A thank you to my family, Miles and Coco, and especially to Todd for his encouragement and support that makes this crazy life possible, to Susan Schuman and Robert Stone my business partners, to the team at Stone Yamashita Partners who never cease to amaze, to the CEOs over the years who have inspired us (Carly Fiorina, Meg Whitman, Paul Pressler, Pat Mitchell, Harlan Bratcher, Lou Gerstner, Michael Jackson, Larry Miller, Steven P. Jobs, Mike Volkema, Elizabeth Birch, John Podesta, Robert Redford, Dave Coulter, among others). And also to the brilliant people along the way who've taught me much (in no particular or symbolic order): Andy Dreyfus, Diane Harwood, Debra Dunn, Randy Komisar, Bill McDonough, Paul Rand, Ivy Ross, Hugh Dubberly, Clement Mok, Cathy Cook, Polly LaBarre, Gary VanSpronsen, Doris Mitsch, Lisa Maulhardt, Tom Andrews, Greg Parsons, Liz Sutton, Sue Adelhardt, Jim March, C.J. Maupin, Paul Pangaro, Michael Tchao, Eames Demetrios (and the whole Eames clan), Jon Iwata, Jana Weatherbee, Mike Wing, Terry Yoo, Mark Harris, Melinda McMullen, Gary Briggs, Annette Goodwine, Ann Livermore, Eva Sage-Gavin, Jenny Ming, Marka Hansen, Gary Muto, Anne Gust, Byron Pollitt, Toby Lenk, Steve Hayden, Mike Paxson, Karen Jorgensen, Kit Mura-Smith, Barbara Waugh, Ric Grefé, Beth Comstock, Susan Peters, Bob Corcoran, George Anderson, Laura Nichols, Alan Webber, Marc Mathieu, Esther Lee, Penny McIntyre, David Butler, Daniel Rosenblum, Ruri Kawashima, Betty Borden, Makiko Sato, Hannah Jones, Alan Marks, Gabriella Rossi, Becca Rees and Alex Ashton, among many, many others who I should thank. And a very special thank you to Allison Johnson, whose constant challenges combined with inherent faith have enabled me to achieve things I would have never dared to attempt on my own.

Sandy would like to thank: As this book's original incarnation and primary purpose was as a teaching tool, I am most grateful to my MBA students at Yale for the rigor and enthusiasm with which they approach their studies. I also extend my ongoing appreciation to the organizations I have studied personally or worked with as a consultant; I am grateful, as a researcher first and foremost, for opportunities to extend and apply my knowledge in the varied and challenging settings they present. I owe a debt of gratitude to many in academia who have influenced my thinking and teaching: Jennifer Chatman, Barry Staw, Glenn Carroll, Jim Lincoln, David Levine, Jennifer Berdahl, Sigal Barsade, Victor Vroom, Don Gibson, Jennifer Mueller, Jim March, Joanne Martin, Dick Scott, Bob Sutton, Joseph Berger, Bernie Cohen, and the many others who have provided valuable insights along the way. I am in awe of the teams at Stone Yamashita Partners and ZipFly for their tremendous abilities and commitment. Finally, my deepest gratitude is reserved for my friends and family; they make all the difference.

Thanks to the following photographers for incredible images: Chris Buck, Bill Gallery, Sian Kennedy, and Greg Miller.